Great Food Without Fuss

Also by Frances McCullough

Holiday Home Cooking
Earth, Air, Fire, and Water
Love Is Like the Lion's Tooth
Sylvia Plath's Journals

GREAT FOOD WITHOUT FUSS

SIMPLE RECIPES FROM THE BEST COOKS

Frances McCullough and Barbara Witt

HENRY HOLT AND COMPANY · NEW YORK

Copyright © 1992 by Frances McCullough and Barbara Witt

All rights reserved, including the right to reproduce this book or portions thereof in any form.

Published by Henry Holt and Company, Inc., 115 West 18th Street, New York, New York 10011.

Published in Canada by Fitzhenry & Whiteside Limited, 91 Granton Drive,
Richmond Hill, Ontario L4B 2N5.

Library of Congress Cataloging-in-Publication Data
McCullough, Frances Monson.
p.   cm.   Includes index.
1. Quick and easy cookery.   I. Witt, Barbara.   II. Title.
TX833.5.M43   1992   92-8473
641.5 12—dc20   CIP
ISBN 0-8050-2230-9

Henry Holt books are available at special discounts for bulk purchases for sales promotions,
premiums, fund-raising, or educational use. Special editions or book excerpts
can also be created to specification.
For details contact: Special Sales Director, Henry Holt and Company, Inc.,
115 West 18th Street, New York, New York 10011.

First Edition—1992

DESIGNED BY LUCY ALBANESE
ILLUSTRATIONS BY ARLENE COOPER

Printed in the United States of America
Recognizing the importance of preserving the written word,
Henry Holt and Company, Inc., by policy, prints all
of its first editions on acid-free paper. ∞

3   5   7   9   10   8   6   4   2

Contents

Introduction

This book grew out of many hours of passionate talk about food between two friends who love to cook. One of us is a cookbook editor who's been lucky enough to work with some of the great cooks—Diana Kennedy, Paula Wolfert, and Deborah Madison among them—and the other is a self-taught cook who founded one of the most interesting restaurants Washington, D.C., has ever seen: The Big Cheese in Georgetown. The editor, who's not a particularly inspired cook and has less and less time to devote to the kitchen, had been collecting some favorite recipes, which just happened to be fast and simple, from the best cookbooks. The cook, whose culinary imagination is always in overdrive, was fascinated by these recipes and could immediately think of dozens of ways to play with them—variations, different ways of serving them, little tricks that could speed the process even more.

Both of us agree that we want above all else to eat well, to get dinner on the table every night and to have it be an imaginative, satisfying meal that sustains soul as well as body. And for company, we want to serve memorable meals with a minimum of fuss. It's not just the time in the kitchen we begrudge; it's the concentration, the claim on our total attention that complex food requires. These recipes are not only a snap to put together, they're also forgiving if you don't follow them slavishly. Of course there are dozens of "quick" cookbooks on the market, but we find that recipes developed specifically for speed tend to come up short in taste, usually because they don't allow time for the flavors to deepen and develop. Some of the recipes in this book take what may seem like a long time, but they're all extremely easy in terms of the actual attention you give them. The secret is in perfectly balancing flavors, and that's the province of the great cooks. They are our source for a collection of very simple, unusual recipes and bright ideas that we think other cooks with limited time and big culinary ambitions will find useful.

One look will convince you that this is not an ordinary cookbook; in fact, you can use it in several different ways. The recipes from the experts are designed so that you can use the book simply as a cook's scrapbook. Or you can use our serving suggestions and tips as a basis for your own improvisations. If you want to plan a company dinner, look first at the Main Dish section, which is the heart of the book. Once you have your main dish under control, the rest of the meal is easy to work out. Remember that we are beginning to cross the line between family and company fare—a simple home-cooked meal that's absolutely delicious is a great treat, especially for people who dine out frequently. There are times, of course, when only something extraordinary will do, but even then, the simpler the better. The luxury can all be in the basic ingredients.

Another way in which this isn't an ordinary cookbook: The serving sizes of each dish are extremely variable since they come from so many different sources. Not to worry; all the dishes multiply well, but do check the serving sizes when you're putting together an entire menu from the book so you won't be caught short.

Among the special features of the book are tips we've gathered from the experts over the years. These little tricks are soon forgotten when you read them in a cookbook, but they are invaluable. Another feature is pertinent notes on microwaving. We all have these gizmos, and few of us use them to good advantage. We hope you'll get into the habit, if you aren't already, of thinking of your microwave not as a substitute for your stove but as your personal R2D2 for many kitchen chores. We haven't been too specific about microwave times because they vary from oven to oven, but you'll quickly get the idea.

Because this food is so simple, it doesn't require much fancy equipment. We assume that you have a food processor and a blender. In our kitchens we couldn't do without a zester (to strip the colored peel off citrus fruit in seconds), a hand-held wooden lemon juicer (it looks like a darning egg and saves hauling out the artillery every time you need a little fresh lemon juice), and a Mouli rotary cheese grater. But our hands-down favorite timesaver is the string-pull salad spinner, which dries the greens thoroughly in a matter of moments.

Mainly because we can't restrain ourselves, we've offered some recipes from our own kitchens in the book, favorite dishes we've been cooking for years that can be brought to the table in minutes. And there are also some mini-recipes, such as cocktail snacks that need little or no cooking at all, and dessert tidbits that go with dessert wines.

A cautionary note: Salmonella scares come and go, but if you have the slightest doubt about the safety of your egg supply, pass by the raw egg recipes on pages 39, 55, and 238.

And how did we choose the recipes? We looked in hundreds of cookbooks, tested and tested and tested, and finally it came down to what tasted best to us, tempered, of course, by considerations of balance and availability. Virtually every good cook we know has a similar secret inventory of simple recipes to use in a crunch, the result of years and years in the kitchen. In the end ours is a very personal and quirky collection—we're fond of both old classics that are unsurpassed, like spoon bread and corn fritters, and new exciting tastes that derive from the exotic produce coming into our supermarkets as well as condiments from the far corners of the world. We trust that you, too, have both an adventurous palate and a fondness for the great nostalgic dishes that have appeared on American tables for decades.

Starters

DIPS AND FINGER FOODS

Sweet Pea Guacamole

Cottage Cheese Dip with Garlic and Herbs

Herbed Yogurt Cheese Dip

Anchovies Gremolata

Pepper Boats with Black Bean Puree

Prosciutto and Breadsticks

Salami, Radishes, and Turnips

Smoked Salmon and Cucumbers

Crostini

Potted Spreads

Nuts

SOUPS

Mushroom and Hazelnut Soup

Yellow Squash Soup

Cold Tomato Soup

Fresh Coriander Soup

Cold Buttermilk Soup

Billi Bi

Oyster Avgolemono Soup

SHELLFISH

Piquant Prawns
Bourbon Shrimp
Bay Scallops with Sautéed Apples

PASTA

Pasta with Caviar
Cappellini with Lemon and Basil
Skillet Pasta
Quick Pasta Sauces

VEGETABLES AND SALADS

Avocado with Radishes
Celery Hearts with Peppercorn Dressing
Thai Cucumber Salad
Mushroom and Cheese Salad
Parsley Salad
A Really Good Green Salad
Vinaigrette

$\mathcal{W}$e often hear caterers remark that their clients seem to remember the beginning and end of their meals with great clarity, while the main courses remain a little vague. And there are those who judge a restaurant by the quality and style of the bread and butter, the very first presentation from the kitchen. We've never had a memorable meal that didn't both begin and end very well indeed.

But do you really need to serve an appetizer? Arrigo Cipriani, of the legendary Harry's Bar in Venice, doesn't think so, on the grounds that starters actually dull the appetite. That may be true, but appetizers can be so appealing that many would prefer making an entire meal of them. If you are such a dedicated nibbler, try eliminating the seated first course and offer three or four successive taste-teasers with aperitifs. Good choices would include crisp croustades topped with marinated vegetables, such as roasted peppers, mushrooms, and sundried tomatoes, or bits of previously grilled eggplant, leeks, or red onion. Follow with a smoked fish and/or miniature kebabs of spicy cooked meat. Expand the array with a dish of special olives, or your favorite flavored roasted nut, or one or two of the myriad new "crispies" in the specialty food stores. This approach works particularly well with ethnic meals because it heightens the drama of what follows and allows you to offer a wider range of flavors than the entree alone can present.

The quick dips, spreads, and finger foods at the beginning of this chapter will give you ideas, or possibly just reminders, of simple, tasty nibbles for serving with cocktails, whether there is a starter course or not. The contemporary cliché is the platter of crudités—those lackluster veggies so laboriously prepared and dutifully received. While it's appropriate to offer today's health-conscious guest an alternative to the super-rich canapé, we suggest that the canapé not only pique the appetite but buffer the system against the rapid effect of alcohol. An adventurous selection of a couple of cheeses, perhaps one low-fat Chèvre, would be more effective and palate-pleasing than carrot sticks and celery. Add some interesting vegetables and a dip or two (see page 8). The abundant cheese board with its lavish choice of rich and runny cheeses should be avoided. High-fat cheese is very filling and will dull the meal to follow.

We encourage you to adapt and re-create these recipes just as our expert cooks have done. Several of the appetizers could become entrees or components of a multidish buffet or even a collection of treats for a cocktail buffet. If you have trouble trying to decide if a particular appetizer will be right with a certain main dish, try to visualize it on the same plate and see if it balances out in your imagination. Don't despair when you make mistakes; all of the cooks represented in this book have erred their way to excellence. Most of the time your own improvisations will delight your guests, and the fact that you have personalized the dish will add to their pleasure.

Sweet Pea Guacamole

Michael Roberts

Unlikely as this recipe sounds, it's quite delicious in a completely different way from traditional avocado guacamole. Ripe avocados are often scarce—usually just when you want to make guacamole—but sweet little frozen peas are always in the freezer section at the supermarket, so you can always prepare an appealing substitute.

MAKES 2 CUPS

Combine oil, lime juice, cilantro, and jalapeño in a blender or food processor and blend until cilantro and hot pepper are roughly pureed. Add peas, cumin, and salt and blend until smooth. There will still be some lumps, but this adds to the textural interest of the guacamole. Scrape into a mixing bowl and add the diced red onion. Serve as a dip with tortilla chips or potato chips.

Serving Suggestions: Not only does this sweet pea mixture make a tasty dip with the ubiquitous corn chip, it is ideal as a side dish on the Mexican buffet table because, unlike the real thing, it doesn't quickly lose its appetizing green color. For the same reason it also works well on dishes that call for a guacamole garnish.

Variation: Use more jalapeños and cilantro for a livelier dip.

2 tablespoons virgin olive oil
2 tablespoons fresh lime juice
¼ bunch cilantro, trimmed of long stems
1 jalapeño pepper, seeded, or 2 serrano peppers, seeded
1 pound frozen peas, thawed
¼ teaspoon ground cumin
¾ teaspoon salt
¼ medium red onion, finely diced

DIPS

Everyone still loves the classic sour cream Fifties' dips, whether they admit it or not. Try making these dips a bit more contemporary by using cottage cheese or yogurt as the base. We think you'll agree that these versions lack nothing in flavor or seeming richness. Serve them with interesting raw vegetables—baby turnips, snow peas, endive leaves, strips of different colored bell peppers, or sticks of fennel, kohlrabi, or jicama.

Cottage Cheese Dip with Garlic and Herbs

Process 4 large garlic cloves with 1 cup parsley leaves and 8 to 10 trimmed scallions until finely minced. Add to the mixture 1 cup cottage cheese and ¼ cup light sour cream. Process until smooth. Add salt and pepper to taste. Serve with toasted pita bread triangles.

Herbed Yogurt Cheese Dip

Drain 2 cups yogurt in a sieve set over a bowl in the refrigerator for 8 hours or overnight. Stir in minced fresh herbs and pressed fresh or roasted garlic puree to taste.

COCKTAIL FINGER FOOD

These are tasty, no-fuss tidbits, many of them based on ingredients you usually keep on hand. They'd all go well with a dish of interesting olives or a plate of paper-thin slices of aged Parmesan.

Anchovies Gremolata

We know: Everyone you know hates anchovies—but they'll love these. The trick is to soak the anchovies (canned Spanish or Italian fillets) in milk for 30 minutes to sweeten them. Then pat the anchovies dry and arrange them like the spokes of a wheel on a serving platter. For each 2½-ounce can of anchovies, mince 1 garlic clove and a handful of parsley very fine and fluff together with the grated zest of 1 lemon to make a gremolata. Drizzle extra virgin olive oil over the anchovy fillets and scatter the gremolata over them. Serve with toasted bread triangles and sharp cocktail forks or toothpicks to spear the anchovies.

Pepper Boats with Black Bean Puree

Cut fresh red, green, and yellow bell peppers into long, slender "boats," following the natural ribbing of the vegetable. Take out the seeds and ribs, trim down any very thick tops, and fill with bean puree. For 4 medium bell peppers, in the food processor puree 2 cups well-rinsed and drained canned black beans (1-pound can) with 2 minced or roasted garlic cloves, 1 or 2 seeded and chopped pickled jalapeño peppers, and ¼ cup minced onion or scallion. Add enough sour cream to loosen the mixture and spoon some down the length of each pepper boat. If you like, zap the boats in the microwave for a couple of minutes, just long enough to take away the raw edge from the peppers and heat the beans. In that case, some shredded cheese on top would be great. Freeze any leftover bean mixture for another time.

If you prefer, use canned white beans or cannellini. Proceed as for black beans but substitute ⅓ cup chopped fresh herbs (thyme, marjoram, and/or parsley) for the jalapeños and use olive oil instead of sour cream to loosen the puree. Top with capers or shredded white tuna (albacore).

Prosciutto and Breadsticks

Wrap a half slice of paper-thin prosciutto around one end of a grissini (thin breadstick). Rest the sticks around the rim of a serving platter, ham ends to the center, leaving a circle to fill with black and green Italian olives and/or chunks of raw fennel.

Salami, Radishes, and Turnips

Find a good Italian hard salami or garlicky cervelat and have it peeled and sliced paper thin. Put a dot of chive cream cheese in the center of each slice and fold the salami over in half and again in quarters, using the cream cheese as the glue, to make an easy morsel to pick up. Or spread each slice and roll it up like a cigarette. Arrange the salami on a serving platter with radishes, either cut crosswise into fans and crisped in ice water for at least 1 hour or left plain with a tiny touch of the green top. Include baby white turnips when available; they are sweet and delicious raw, dipped in salt. Add some raw kohlrabi, peeled and cut into sticks and dipped in salt.

Smoked Salmon and Cucumbers

Mix minced smoked salmon trimmings with cream cheese and chives to taste. Cut a cucumber crosswise into ¼-inch slices, mound the salmon mixture on top, and decorate with a sprig of fresh dill.

Crostini

These small rounds of oiled, seasoned toasted bread make wonderful canapés with drinks. You can buy them in specialty shops under several labels. Better yet, make your own. Cut a French baguette into ½-inch rounds, brush both sides with olive oil, and lay out on a cookie sheet. Bake until crisp at 300°. Be certain the crostini are crisp all the way through. Toppings can be as simple as cheese (Chèvre and herbs, fontina and prosciutto, Brie and almonds) melted under the broiler or in the microwave, or as complex as grilled eggplant pureed with onion and sweet red pepper. If you keep a jar of black olive paste on your shelf, you can just spread some on the crostini and serve.

Potted Spreads

A crock of piquant buttery spread is always welcome. Use just enough unsalted butter to carry the seasonings and to make a spreadable paste (about 3 tablespoons but-ter to 1 cup fish or meat cubes). Process until smooth but not homogenized. Taste and adjust seasonings. If you want to make the spread well ahead, simply pour a thin film of melted butter over the top to seal it from the air. Store covered in the refrigerator for about 1 week. Some good combinations are:

- Cooked shrimp with fresh dill and a touch of mustard

- Smoked trout and toasted hazelnuts (delicious spread on apple slices dipped in lemon juice)

- Smoked chicken with sun-dried tomato and minced scallion

- Ham with garlic, parsley, and a dash of brandy or port

- Gorgonzola and walnuts

- Roast beef with horseradish

- Cremini mushrooms sautéed with fresh herbs and dry sherry (wring the mushrooms dry in a clean dish towel after sautéing)

*N*uts are the easiest finger food of all. Here are some ways to dress them up for special occasions.

Nuts

- Toasted pecan halves dipped in Roquefort mixed with cream cheese

- Macadamia nuts mixed with candied ginger and chunks of fresh coconut

- Salted peanuts mixed with minced dried apples

- Black walnuts mixed with minced dried apricots

- Pecans or cashews roasted in curry butter at 350° for 15 to 20 minutes, salted and cooled (keep in a covered container until ready to serve)

- Brazil nuts wrapped with strips of prosciutto

• S O U P S •

Mushroom and Hazelnut Soup

Joyce Goldstein

1 cup hazelnuts
4 tablespoons unsalted butter
6 cups sliced onions
14 cups, loosely packed, fresh white or
    brown mushrooms, cut in chunks
    (or left whole if small)
5 cups chicken stock
1 teaspoon salt
¼ teaspoon freshly ground pepper
Chopped fresh parsley, for garnish

Mushroom soup can be sublime or disappointingly flat, depending mainly on the quality of the mushrooms. Not this one, though; this singular combination is always rich, complex, and elegant.

SERVES 8

Preheat the oven to 350°. Toast the hazelnuts on a baking sheet until the skins crack a little, then rub them in a kitchen towel to remove as much of the skins as possible. Don't be disheartened if you can't get them clean for a little skin won't hurt the soup. Grind the nuts in a food processor and set aside.

Melt the butter in a large deep saucepan over medium heat. Add the onions and cook until tender and translucent, about 10 minutes. Add the mushrooms and sweat them, covered, about 5 minutes. Add enough chicken stock to barely cover and heat to boiling. Reduce the heat and simmer about 10 minutes.

Puree the mushrooms and onions with the nuts and a little of the hot stock in batches in a blender or food processor. Thin the soup to the desired consistency with hot stock. Season with salt and pepper and garnish with chopped fresh parsley, if desired. This soup can be made ahead of time and gently reheated. Thin it with chicken stock if it thickens too much.

Serving Suggestions: This is the ideal starter for a pristine sautéed chicken breast or roast chicken main course. The addition of sherry or marsala and cream makes the soup worthy of a holiday feast of turkey, ham, or roast beef.

Note: Brown mushrooms, Romans or cremini, are usually found in the supermarket packaged like the white ones. They have a more intense flavor and more character than the white, and we tend to use them in all recipes calling for cultivated mushrooms.

Fourteen cups of chopped mushrooms will be a little less than 2½ pounds. Quarter the mushrooms if they're not small.

Variation: Add a jigger of sherry or marsala mixed with cream.

Tip: From Julia Child: If you're slicing or chopping onions, refrigerate them first—no more tears.

Yellow Squash Soup

Diane Rossen Worthington

1 tablespoon olive oil

1½ pounds yellow crookneck squash, shredded

2 tablespoons finely chopped chives

3½ cups chicken stock

1 tablespoon fresh lemon juice

½ cup sour cream

¼ teaspoon salt

¼ teaspoon white pepper

GARNISH

¼ cup sour cream

1 tablespoon finely chopped chives

Yellow crookneck squash may seem an unexciting base for a soup—but this soup is not only sunny and cheerful-looking, it's also delicate and delicious. It can be served hot as well as cold, and you can make it a day ahead if you like; the flavors will improve.

SERVES 4 TO 6

Heat the olive oil in a medium saucepan over medium heat. Add the shredded squash and chives and sauté until just softened, about 3 minutes.

Add the chicken stock and simmer for about 5 minutes.

Place in a blender or food processor fitted with a steel blade and process until pureed. Refrigerate until cool.

Whisk in the lemon juice, sour cream, salt, and pepper until well combined. Taste for seasoning.

To serve, ladle the soup into bowls and garnish with the sour cream and chives.

Serving Suggestions: This soup is not assertively spiced, so it makes a particularly refreshing starter for a spicy summer dinner. It would also be just right served before a chicken or seafood salad.

Tips:

If homemade chicken stock is beyond you, substitute canned chicken stock. Get one that's labeled low-sodium; it will also have fewer additives.

From Julia Child: For a mock homemade stock, simmer 3 cups canned chicken broth, ½ cup canned beef bouillon, and ¼ cup dry white wine or vermouth with ¼ cup each minced carrots, celery, and onion, for 30 minutes on top of the stove or 10 minutes, covered, in the microwave. Strain before using.

We've been making this sensational curried tomato soup ever since it first appeared in the 1961 edition of the New York Times Cookbook.

SERVES 5 TO 6

$\mathcal{M}$ix all the ingredients except the sour cream and parsley, adding sugar to taste. Chill.

Before serving, blend in the sour cream and sprinkle each portion with parsley.

Serving Suggestions: A light, spicy cold tomato soup can be served before almost any entree unless it has similar ingredients. On a hot summer evening it would nicely round out a chicken salad main course.

Tips:
Whisk 1 cup of the soup into the sour cream, then blend the mixture into the rest of the soup for a smoother blend.

Use yogurt instead of sour cream for a low-fat version.

Variations:
Trade the tomato juice for V-8, one of the few supermarket miracles in a can.

Substitute ground cumin for curry powder and thyme. Mash garlic cloves into the mixture and add Tabasco to taste. Garnish the soup with minced cilantro and cubes of ripe avocado tossed with lime juice.

Cold Tomato Soup

Craig Claiborne

3 cups tomato juice
2 tablespoons tomato paste
4 scallions, minced
Salt to taste
Pinch of powdered thyme
½ teaspoon curry powder
Freshly ground pepper
Grated zest of ½ lemon
2 tablespoons lemon juice
Sugar
1 cup sour cream
Chopped parsley

Fresh Coriander Soup
(Sopa de coentro)

Jean Anderson

This zesty soup is for cilantro (fresh coriander) addicts like our-selves, but be warned—people either love cilantro or loathe it. So this isn't the right soup to serve strangers or anyone whose cilantro opinion you don't know. Remember to make the soup a day ahead. Serve it hot or cold. Aside from the generous addition of cilantro, this is a basic potato soup, without cream, which you can vary innumerable ways. If cilantro isn't a partic-ular favorite of yours, experiment using other herbs in combi-nations that please you.

SERVES 6 TO 8

4 medium yellow onions, peeled and
    coarsely chopped
2 large garlic cloves, peeled and
    minced
4 tablespoons olive oil
4 medium potatoes, peeled and
    coarsely chopped
6 cups rich chicken broth, preferably
    homemade
Salt to taste
¼ teaspoon cayenne pepper
¾ cup coarsely chopped fresh corian-
    der leaves (1 large bunch)

In a large heavy saucepan set over moderate heat, sauté the onions and garlic in 3 tablespoons of the olive oil 5 minutes until limp; add the remaining tablespoon of oil and the potatoes and stir-fry 1 minute. Add the broth, cover, and simmer 45 minutes until the potatoes are mushy. Remove from the heat and puree, about a fourth of the total amount at a time, by buzzing 60 seconds in a food processor fitted with the metal chopping blade or in an electric blender. If you have neither processor nor blender, simply force all through a fine sieve. Pour the soup into a large heatproof bowl, stir in salt if needed, the cayenne, and the coriander. Cover and refrigerate 24 hours. Serve cold, or pour into a large heavy saucepan, set over moderate heat, and bring slowly to a simmer. Ladle into soup plates and serve hot.

Serving Suggestions: A sturdy herbal soup like this one is best served before a simple fish entree or even as the entree itself, followed by a salad. If your family likes cilantro, serve the soup with a platter of cheese, chicken and tomato nachos, or Enchiladas Suizas (page 83).

Tip: Cook the potato mixture in the microwave to save some time.

Variations:

Substitute parsley and chives for the cilantro; they will give the cold version a lovely fresh garden flavor. In that case, substitute light cream for some of the stock to enrich the flavor.

Stir pesto into the soup instead of cilantro, starting with ¼ cup and tasting as you go to hit the right balance.

For a bright green summer soup, puree lightly steamed spinach along with the potatoes and use 4 cups chicken stock and 2 cups light cream, half-and-half, or yogurt.

Make the spinach soup as in the previous variation, but instead of cream use 2 cups well-drained, pureed canned Italian plum tomatoes. Spike the soup with a little ground cumin and 1 or 2 seeded and minced jalapeño peppers. Stir in the jalapeño just before serving.

Substitute carrots or parsnips for half the potatoes and season with curry powder mixed with a few drops of oil and cooked briefly in the microwave to release its flavor. Watch the quantity of cayenne if your curry powder is hot.

Cold Buttermilk Soup

M. F. K. Fisher

Mrs. Fisher writes: "This is one of my growing number of Things I Do Not Mention Gastronomically. If I tell the smiling people who sip at it that it is made of mashed shrimps and especially buttermilk, they wince, gag, hurry away. So I say nothing and serve it from invisible hogsheads to unconscious but happy hordes." Just so. We love this soup and make it several times each summer, but our guests always give us a fishy eye when we tell them what's in it.

SERVES 6

1½ pounds shrimp, cooked and
    chopped
1 medium cucumber, finely diced
1 tablespoon minced fresh dill
1 tablespoon prepared mustard
1 teaspoon salt
1 teaspoon sugar
1 quart buttermilk

Mix together shrimp, cucumber, and seasonings. Stir in buttermilk and chill thoroughly.

Serving Suggestions: This versatile soup would be a fine starter for any summer main course that doesn't involve a cream sauce.

Variations:
You can also make a version of the soup without shrimp. Grate 2 cucumbers and 1 small onion. Mix 1 cup sour cream with the vegetables, mix the mustard with the sugar, then combine the two. Add the buttermilk. Chill for several hours. Before serving, grind a little pepper on top.

Sprinkle chopped dill or parsley or snipped chives on top of the soup.

Billi Bi

Craig Claiborne after Pierre Franey

Not only is this one of the most luxurious soups ever conceived, it's also inexpensive, easy to prepare, and versatile. You can serve it hot or cold.

SERVES 4

2 pounds mussels
2 shallots, coarsely chopped
2 small onions, quartered
2 sprigs of parsley
Salt and freshly ground black pepper
Pinch of cayenne pepper
1 cup dry white wine
2 tablespoons butter
¼ bay leaf
½ teaspoon thyme
2 cups heavy cream
1 egg yolk, lightly beaten

Scrub the mussels well to remove all exterior sand and dirt. Place them in a large kettle with the shallots, onions, parsley, salt, black pepper, cayenne, wine, butter, bay leaf, and thyme. Cover and bring to a boil. Simmer 5 to 10 minutes, or until the mussels have opened. Discard any mussels that do not open.

Strain the liquid through a double thickness of cheesecloth. Reserve the mussels for another use or remove them from the shells and use them as a garnish.

Bring the liquid in the saucepan to a boil and add the cream. Return to the boil and remove from the heat. Add the beaten egg yolk and return to the heat long enough for the soup to thicken slightly. Do not boil. Serve hot or cold. This dish may be enriched, if desired, by stirring 2 tablespoons of hollandaise sauce into the soup before it is served.

Serving Suggestions: This soup is incredibly rich, so pair it with a spartan main course, such as Great Roast Chicken (pages 71 and 72) or Cornish Hens (page 77). Mussels and poultry marry very well. Try the soup with Chicken Broiled with Mustard, Herbs, and Bread Crumbs (page 63).

Tips:
Save the mussels for a lovely salad bound with a saffron-flavored mayonnaise with chives; remember, mussels

combine well with scallops if you'd like to extend the salad.

The mussels will keep 3 to 4 days, well covered and refrigerated.

Oyster Avgolemono Soup

James Villas

4 egg yolks
Juice of 2 lemons
1½ pints shucked oysters, drained,
    liquor reserved
4 cups chicken stock or broth
¼ cup orzo pasta
Salt and freshly ground pepper
Tabasco
2 sprigs of parsley, chopped

This sensational soup should really motivate you to keep homemade chicken stock in your freezer. The addition of the elegant oysters to the peasant soup is brilliant.

SERVES 6

Place egg yolks in a medium mixing bowl, whisk till creamy, add lemon juice, and whisk till well blended.

Combine reserved oyster liquor and chicken stock in a large saucepan, bring to the boil, and gradually add orzo. Reduce heat, cover, and simmer for 15 minutes or till pasta is tender. Add salt, pepper, and Tabasco to taste and stir.

Whisk ½ cup hot stock very gradually into egg mixture, add oysters to stock in saucepan, and gradually whisk egg mixture into stock. Heat well but do not boil soup, and stir in chopped parsley.

Serving Suggestions: This is an ideal first course for a holiday meal. Since it's such a soothing soup, you might also consider it for a late supper, with a simple green salad and a crusty bread.

Tip: Follow the recipe directions for adding the egg mixture (last paragraph); the soup will be smooth and velvety.

Variation: Substitute poached scallops, jumbo lump crab-meat, or tiny Greenland shrimp for the oysters. Serve hot or cold. When chilled, blend in a cup of heavy cream or swirl some crème fraîche on top of each serving and garnish with grated lemon zest mixed with the parsley.

• SHELLFISH •

Piquant Prawns
(Gambas picantes)

Madhur Jaffrey after Glenda Barretto

These fiery prawns are a Filipino dish with Spanish origins. You can turn the prawns into a main course by serving them over steamed basmati rice.

SERVES 6 AS A FIRST COURSE
OR 4 AS A MAIN COURSE

Peel and devein the prawns. Wash them, pat them dry, and put them in a bowl. Add the paprika and toss. Peel the garlic and chop it finely. Chop the chilies finely. Put the oil in a wok or large frying pan and set it over a high heat. When the oil is hot, put in the garlic. Stir-fry for 30 seconds, or until the garlic turns golden. Put in the prawns and green chilies. Stir-fry over a high heat for 2 to 3 minutes, or until the prawns turn opaque all the way through. Add the salt and pepper. Toss again and serve.

1 pound uncooked, unpeeled prawns
1 teaspoon paprika
5 garlic cloves
1 or 2 fresh hot green chilies
4 tablespoons olive oil
½ teaspoon salt
Freshly ground black pepper

Serving Suggestions: Serve the prawns heaped on a platter. They are especially good with an ethnic main course: Serve a small portion before Roast Pork with Bay Leaves (page 97), for example. Or serve them before herbed Cornish Hen (page 77) or a charcoal-grilled veal chop.

Variations:

Where prawns are unavailable substitute jumbo or large shrimp.

You can defuse the heat by substituting minced green pepper for the chilies.

Charcoal-grill the peeled prawns, keeping their tails intact.

Use Thai chili sauce, Chinese chili paste, or your favorite bottled hot sauce in place of fresh chilies.

Bourbon Shrimp

Amy Ferguson

1 pound prawns or jumbo shrimp
2 tablespoons unsalted butter
½ cup bourbon
2 teaspoons tomato paste
1 cup heavy cream
1 tablespoon chopped fresh dill
Salt and white pepper to taste
Additional sprigs of dill for garnish

The sweetness of the shrimp is accentuated by the bourbon, and the addition of the dilled tomato cream makes a perfect contrast. Since sauced appetizers cool off quickly, serve the shrimp piled on rounds of toasted French bread to keep them warm and to catch every bit of sauce.

SERVES 4 TO 6

Peel the shrimp and devein them. Wash under cold running water and pat them dry with paper toweling.

In a sauté pan or skillet, heat the butter over medium-high heat until sizzling and add the prawns. Sauté for 1 minute, until they just begin to turn pink, and add the bourbon. Raise the heat to high and sauté until the liquid is reduced to a few tablespoons, about 1 minute.

Add the tomato paste and cream, and continue to cook for 1 minute. Remove the shrimp or prawns from the pan with a slotted spoon and set them aside to keep warm. Reduce the sauce by half, then add the chopped dill and season with salt and pepper to taste.

Spoon the sauce over the shrimp and garnish with additional sprigs of fresh dill.

Serving Suggestions: This dish would be a good starter before a pristine sautéed fish, such as fillets of flounder, grouper, or catfish. Accompany the fish fillets with Hot Devil Potatoes (page 175) and follow with a mixed green salad with ripe tomatoes and crumbled feta.

Variations:

If you like the taste of aquavit, use it instead of bourbon for a Scandinavian-style version of this dish. Add a little grated fresh horseradish to the cream in place of the dill.

This recipe would make a fine sauce for a main-dish fish fillet or even a skinned, poached chicken breast. Use tiny shrimp or medium ones cut in half lengthwise. Adjust the recipe to allow 3 or 4 shrimp per serving.

Bay Scallops with Sautéed Apples

Wolfgang Puck

This is one of those unusual California fruit and fish combinations that really works. And it's very pretty.

SERVES 6

2 Pippin or Granny Smith apples
2 tablespoons unsalted butter
1 pound fresh baby bay scallops
Salt
Freshly ground white pepper
1 tablespoon almond or safflower oil
1 tablespoon chopped fresh Italian parsley or cilantro

Peel, halve, and core the apples. Slice them thinly or cut them into ¼-inch julienne strips.

Heat a large sauté pan and add the butter. In it sauté the apples over moderate heat 2 to 3 minutes, or until they are slightly brown but still crispy. It is better to sauté the apples (and scallops) in several small batches than to crowd your sauté pan.

Season the scallops with salt and pepper. Heat another large sauté pan and add the oil. In it sauté the scallops over high heat until just springy to the touch, from 30 seconds to 1 minute, depending on their size. Remove from the heat.

Stir in the parsley or cilantro and correct the seasonings.

Arrange the apple slices in a wreath on warm appetizer plates and place the scallops in the center of the wreaths. Garnish with sprigs of Italian parsley or cilantro.

Serving Suggestions: Scallops are light and make a good company first course before poultry, veal, pork, or ham.

Pasta with Caviar
(Pasta con caviale)

Fred Plotkin

This is a very luxurious way to begin an elegant meal. It also appeals to us as a late supper treat after an evening out, accompanied by a flute of champagne. It isn't necessary to buy the best caviar you can find; try it with a jar of Danish lumpfish caviar, which is neither strong nor salty. Grate a tiny amount of onion into the butter.

SERVES 2

3 tablespoons unsalted butter
¼ cup heavy cream
8 ounces spaghettini or taglialini
1 ounce fresh caviar

Set a large pot of cold water to boil. When the water reaches a full boil, toss in a pinch of salt.

In a saucepan, melt the butter over low heat until foamy and add the cream. At this point start cooking the pasta. When the cream and butter are well blended, add the caviar and continue to stir gently. When the pasta is al dente, drain and transfer to a warm dish. Add the sauce, toss well, and serve.

Serving Suggestions: Try this before Veal Scallops with Fennel (page 93) or Rolled Stuffed Turkey Cutlets (page 81).

Cappellini with Lemon and Basil

Deborah Madison

Lightly sauced herbal or seafood pastas, served in very small portions, are welcome starters for company dinners. They are uncomplicated and effortless to prepare. This dish is both lively and delicate.

Zest of 1 lemon, cut into narrow
　　strips
Juice of 1 lemon
1½ tablespoons unsalted butter
1½ tablespoons extra virgin olive oil
8 fresh basil leaves, finely sliced
2 teaspoons finely chopped parsley
3 ounces cappellini
Salt
Freshly ground pepper
Freshly grated Parmigiano-Reggiano,
　　if desired

SERVES 2

Put the lemon zest, juice, butter, oil, and herbs in a bowl large enough to hold the cooked pasta comfortably. Also have ready 2 heated pasta bowls or plates.

Bring several quarts of water to a boil, add salt to taste and the pasta, and cook until al dente. Lift out the noodles with a pasta scoop and add them immediately to the large bowl. Repeatedly lift the noodles with a pair of tongs, mixing them with the other ingredients as you do so. Divide the pasta between the 2 bowls and add a little pepper. Serve with cheese, if desired.

Serving Suggestions: Serve this before leg of lamb or Grilled Swordfish with Mustard (page 58). A vegetable accompaniment like Asparagus Poêlé (page 134) and a salad to follow would be sufficient since starter pastas eliminate the need for a second starch.

Variations:
Top the cappellini with a few small shrimp quickly sautéed in butter and olive oil with minced garlic and a few crushed red pepper flakes.

Add tiny poached bay scallops, oysters, or baby clams with crumbled crisp bacon. Substitute fresh mint for the basil.

Ring each dish with 3 or 4 steamed mussels in their shells.

Add some crème fraîche or reduced heavy cream to enrich the dish.

EDITORS' KITCHEN

PASTA

Pasta is best when cooked just before serving, of course, but if you can't manage that, there are alternatives. You can cook the pasta ahead of time and reheat it with a simple sauce in a skillet or in the microwave.

Skillet Pasta

Cook and drain the pasta. With your hands or tongs, thoroughly but lightly coat the strands with olive oil to prevent them from sticking together as the pasta cools. Set the pasta aside, uncovered, until you're ready to complete the dish. When you're ready to serve, heat the sauce ingredients in a large skillet and add the pasta, lifting and mixing with tongs to distribute the sauce. Flip the pasta in the skillet, lifting it with tongs to get it very hot, but not steamed. Scatter herbs into the pasta off the heat so they won't turn dark. Serve the pasta right away on hot plates.

Or place the sauce ingredients and pasta in a microwaveable container and cover with wax paper instead of a lid. Reheat in the microwave at 2-minute intervals on High. Lift and loosen the pasta with tongs as you go; stop when the pasta is just hot.

Quick Pasta Sauces

Here are a few of our favorite quick starter pasta sauces:

• Smoked salmon cut in 2-inch strips, butter, reduced cream, and freshly ground black pepper

- Roasted garlic puree or finely minced fresh garlic, olive oil, capers, pitted Italian black olives cut in strips, minced fresh (or dried) oregano, hot-pepper flakes, and Italian flat-leaf parsley

- Chèvre melted in heavy cream (2 ounces Chèvre and ¼ cup heavy cream per serving), garnished with toasted pine nuts or walnuts and chopped basil or parsley

- Anchovies mashed with roasted garlic puree (drain and soak the anchovies in milk for 30 minutes first and drain again), soft unsalted butter, and enough sun-dried tomato paste, if you have it, to turn it pink; sprinkled with chopped parsley

- Slivered mushrooms and garlic sautéed in butter and oil with a pinch of dried thyme and a dash of cayenne, and deglazed with Madeira or vermouth; sprinkled with snipped chives

- Red, green, and yellow bell peppers, julienned and sautéed lightly with garlic in olive oil

•VEGETABLES AND SALADS•

EDITORS' KITCHEN

Avocado with Radishes

This unusual combination of tastes and textures, with the crunchy, spicy radish playing against the creamy, soft avocado, is simplicity itself. Serve it before the first grilled fish or chicken of the season, accompanied by a big glass bowl of creamy potato salad accented with tiny green peas. Look for perfectly ripe avocados of the California Haas variety, with black pebbly skin; they have a good nutty flavor.

FOR EACH SERVING

ℬrush ½ avocado, seeded and peeled, with lemon juice and sprinkle with salt. Toss 3 shredded or julienned white radishes with more lemon juice and let marinate in the refrigerator for about 1 hour. Add 1 tablespoon snipped chives to the radishes and mix well. Fill the avocado cavity with the mixture and decorate with 1 or 2 chive blossoms if you have them.

Variations:

Brush the avocado with fresh lime juice mixed with grated fresh ginger instead of lemon juice.

Substitute daikon for the white radishes, allowing 2 inches of daikon per serving.

Decorate with fresh-picked violets or other edible flowers instead of chive blossoms.

From novelist Len Deighton, who is also a brilliant and knowledgeable cook, comes this easiest-of-all idea, which he swears is the only way to eat an avocado: Pour a big spoonful of Worcestershire sauce into the avocado cavity. Try it with balsamic vinegar.

Celery Hearts with Peppercorn Dressing

Nina Simonds

Celery seems to us far more interesting in its raw state than cooked. Here the celery is quickly blanched to produce a spicy, crispy Chinese celery dish that's served at room temperature.

SERVES 6

2 pounds celery hearts

SPICY PEPPERCORN DRESSING

1 teaspoon freshly ground white
  pepper
¼ cup soy sauce
2 tablespoons sesame oil
2 tablespoons minced scallions
1 tablespoon minced gingerroot
1 tablespoon Chinese black vinegar
2 teaspoons sugar

1 tablespoon minced scallion greens,
  for garnish

Rinse the celery hearts and peel away the tough skin, if any. Trim the ends and cut away any leaves. Cut the celery stalks into 3-inch lengths and then cut crosswise into thin slices about ⅛ inch thick. Heat 2 quarts of water until boiling and drop the celery slices into the boiling water for 30 seconds. Remove and immediately immerse in cold water. Drain thoroughly and pat dry. Place the slices in a large bowl.

To make the spicy peppercorn dressing, heat a dry wok until hot and add the white pepper. Stirring constantly, cook over medium heat for about 1 minute, until fragrant. Transfer to a bowl and add the remaining dressing ingredients. Mix to blend and then add to the celery slices. Toss to coat. Transfer the slices to a serving platter and sprinkle the minced scallions on top. Serve at room temperature.

Serving Suggestions: In China this dish is served as a snack, accompanied by other tidbits, all carefully balanced in color and flavor. You can serve it that way too, of course, but if you're using it as a first course, you might want to add some julienned green or red pepper strips to the celery.

If you're following with an ethnic main course, accompany this appetizer with a couple of steamed shaomai, tender little dumplings stuffed with shrimp and chicken that are now being imported from Hong Kong to supermarket freezers.

Note: The heart is the tender center of the head of celery and is sometimes available packaged separately. Or pull off the outer ribs of the celery until you reach the tender interior.

Variation: Substitute balsamic vinegar if you cannot find Chinese black vinegar.

Thai Cucumber Salad

Leslie Newman

Thai cuisine features many of these simple, sparkling little salads. They are great palate teasers.

SERVES 10 TO 12

*I*n a large bowl, combine the vinegar, sugar, hot red-pepper flakes, and salt. Stir until the sugar is dissolved. Set aside.

Score the cucumbers with a fork and then cut them into ¼-inch slices. Stack the slices and cut into quarters. Add the cucumbers and chopped red onions to the bowl of salad dressing and toss well. Cover and refrigerate for 1 to 4 hours, stirring occasionally.

Just before serving, add the chopped peanuts. Toss the salad once more and serve in small individual bowls.

Serving Suggestions: Serve this salad before Pork Slices with Prunes (page 102), Orange-spiced Chicken Wings

¾ cup distilled white vinegar
⅓ cup sugar, preferably superfine
½ to 1 teaspoon hot red-pepper
  flakes, to taste
¼ teaspoon coarse (kosher) salt
2¼ to 2½ pounds long European-
  style cucumbers, washed and dried
  but not peeled
¼ cup finely chopped red onions
¼ cup chopped salted roasted peanuts

(page 64), or leftover pork roast with chutney (page 101).

Variations:
Add chunks of cooked Chinese sausage. Slice several sausages in half lengthwise, then crosswise into ½-inch slices. Fry over low heat (or broil) until cooked through, about 4 minutes. Drain and garnish with chopped fresh cilantro. Omit the peanuts.

Substitute rice wine vinegar for the distilled white vinegar; it's less sharp.

Mushroom and Cheese Salad

(Insalata di funghi e formaggio)

Marcella Hazan

½ pound very crisp, white fresh
    mushrooms
Juice of ½ lemon
⅔ cup Swiss cheese cut into strips
    1 inch long, ¼ inch wide, and
    ⅛ inch thick
3 tablespoons olive oil
Salt to taste
Freshly ground pepper, a liberal
    quantity, to taste

Reminiscent of the wild mushroom, truffle, and cheese salads of the Italian Alps, the woodsy combination of raw mushrooms and cheese is an appealing beginning to virtually any meal.

SERVES 4

Detach the mushroom stems from the caps. Save the stems for another recipe. Wipe the caps clean with a damp cloth, then cut into slices ⅛ inch thick. Put the slices in a salad bowl and moisten them with some lemon juice to keep them from discoloring. (You can prepare these as much as 30 to 45 minutes ahead of time.)

When ready to serve, add the strips of Swiss cheese to the bowl and toss with the olive oil, salt, and pepper.

Serving Suggestions: Serve this salad atop a paper-thin slice or two of prosciutto, or nest the mushrooms and cheese in a bed of arugula and place two thin breadsticks on the plate, each one wrapped in a half slice of prosciutto.

Variations:

If you are lucky enough to receive a bottle of Italian truffle oil as a gift, use it on this salad, stretching it out by combining it with an equal measure of light olive oil or safflower oil.

For a very special dinner, choose a combination of fresh wild mushrooms that can be eaten raw, such as porcini, oyster mushrooms, shiitake, or enoki. Or mix brown cremini with cultivated white mushrooms for a more intense flavor.

French chef Joel Robuchon makes a similar salad using the same quantities of mushrooms, oil, and lemon juice, adding a finely minced garlic clove and a bundle of snipped fresh herbs—parsley, basil, tarragon, and thyme. Just tarragon and parsley work fine, though. Robuchon substitutes shaved Parmesan for the Swiss cheese. As always, we prefer cremini mushrooms here.

EDITORS' KITCHEN

This refreshing salad is one of those California inspirations that seem to have been passed around from chef to chef, restaurant to restaurant. We think it originated at Café Beaujolais in Mendocino. Now there are many versions, but we like this simple one best. It is particularly good with a grilled main dish or an Italian-style entree, such as the Succulent Pork Roast with

Parsley Salad

Fennel (page 99). For us, curly parsley works best in this dish, but others prefer the Italian flat-leaf. The important thing is for the parsley to be very fresh.

SERVES 4

Mix together ¼ cup extra virgin olive oil, 2 tablespoons fresh lemon juice, 2 pressed garlic cloves, lots of pepper, and salt to taste. Wash 4 cups very fresh parsley leaves (2 bunches) and dry thoroughly in a salad spinner or on towels. Toss the parsley and 4 oil-packed sun-dried tomatoes, drained and julienned, with the dressing, sprinkle with ¼ cup freshly grated Parmesan, and serve immediately.

Variations:
Substitute 1 minced scallion, 1 tablespoon chopped fresh mint, and 2 sliced radishes for the sun-dried tomatoes, and 2 ounces crumbled feta for the Parmesan.

Substitute 2 minced shallots and 8 pitted and slivered kalamata olives for the sun-dried tomatoes, and ¼ cup grated pecorino for the Parmesan.

A Really Good Green Salad

For many people, dinner is not complete without a salad. A perfect green salad is a delight—an interesting leafy bouquet that's always the most natural, unprocessed part of the meal. The right balance of flavor and texture can stimulate or refresh the palate, depending on whether you choose to serve it before or after the main course. Success depends on pristine ingredients, attentive preparation, and good luck—we've all made salads that are technically perfect yet didn't come alive in the bowl. With patience, though, you should be able to taste your way to success. Here's a brief refresher course on preparing a really good salad.

PERFECT GREENS

Any green leafy vegetable that tastes good raw—from lettuce to tiny beet greens—is fair pickings for the salad bowl. For a mixed green salad, select either all light greens, such as leaf, Boston, Bibb, mesclun, and mâche, or mix in one-third heavy greens, such as spinach, escarole, or romaine. Too many heavy greens in a mixed salad will flatten the lighter, fluffy ones and will hold the dressing unevenly. A salad of all heavy greens is a robust course suitable to accompany barbecues or main dish soups and demands a zesty dressing.

Bitter greens, such as curly endive (frisée), Belgian endive, and radicchio, should be used sparingly and in small bites. Some greens, like Bibb and Belgian endive, taste better all by themselves than mixed with other greens. A true minimalist salad is just arugula, dressed only with the best olive oil and salt, and very good it is too.

Prepare the greens as soon as they come into the house. (Washing and trimming the greens before they're stored is an easy habit to get into, and not only will your greens keep longer, you'll be ready to produce a great salad on a moment's notice.) Trim off the stem end with a sharp paring knife—the only time, purists say, you will touch a knife to fresh greens—and discard any imperfect outer leaves or rusty patches. Separate the leaves and rinse them thoroughly under cool running water and then dry them well in a salad spinner (the pull-cord style is best). The greens should be slightly damp to the touch unless you're going to make them into a salad immediately, in which case they should be bone dry. Put the heavier greens in the bottom of a large plastic bag, with the tender varieties on top. Don't mash them down at all. Turn the top of the bag under (don't make it airtight with a twist-tie) and store it in the crisper of your refrigerator. The greens should keep at least a week. When you're ready for salad, all you have to do is make sure the greens are dry and tear them into bite-size pieces. Count on a large handful of greens per person, about two cupfuls.

EMBELLISHMENTS

We prefer the term "embellishments" to "toppings," but toppings are what such things as crumbled smoked bacon, edible flowers, cherry tomatoes (seeded and slivered) are. Cheese, too, is a good embellishment, whether it's grated Parmesan or dry Monterey Jack; crumbled feta, blue, or Roquefort; or grilled or breaded and fried cubes of Chèvre.

Keep your garnishes light and minimal; substantial chunks will flatten a fine salad or sink to the bottom of the plate. Avoid chopped vegetables such as cucumbers, carrots, radishes, green peppers, and celery; they are too heavy for a tossed green salad.

Use slivered scallions or snipped chives rather than raw onion if you want an onion taste. Or pour boiling water over the sliced onions, let them sit for 15 minutes, drain, and dry them—they'll magically sweeten.

Select your embellishments to suit the greens, and think about what goes best with the rest of the meal when you make your choice. Here are a few combinations we like:

- Toasted pine nuts and feta on flat-leaf spinach

- French bread garlic croutons and avocado slices on romaine

- Grilled Chèvre on mesclun and mâche

• Crumbled Gorgonzola and chopped walnuts over pear wedges on dark greens

DINNER PARTY SALADS

Glass plates present a green salad most appealingly, and if you put them in the freezer before dinner, they will not only keep your salad crisp and chilled at the table but also display a pretty frosted edge.

Save the perfect green salad for seated dinner parties. Mixed greens don't fare well on buffet tables. Instead, have what Diana Kennedy calls a ranch salad: tender leaves of romaine fanned out in overlapping concentric circles on a large platter with salad tidbits scattered on top—sliced radishes, slivered scallions, seeded cherry tomato halves, and so on. Serve a thickish dressing in a dish on the side. The leaves can be eaten out of hand, and they'll stay crisp and pretty for a reasonably long time.

Vinaigrette

For a classic vinaigrette, begin with the best possible basic ingredients in a palatable proportion: We think that's four parts oil to one part vinegar or fresh lemon juice. If the vinegar is very sharp or the lemon particularly sour, increase the oil to five parts. But many salad connoisseurs opt for a ratio of three to one or even six to one; you have to taste and decide. The other basics are freshly ground black pepper and, ideally, pure sea salt or Kosher salt. This caveat isn't an affectation; iodized salt isn't disguised in a salad, and other chemical or off-tastes—such as slightly rancid oil, astringent vinegar, sprouted garlic, or bottled lemon juice—are also very obvious.

Olive oil can sometimes be overpowering, so taste yours, and if it is too strong, dilute the robust flavor with up to half safflower or canola oil, which are virtually flavorless.

Freshly squeezed lemon juice is our first choice for the acid balance on a salad of mixed light greens. A mix of mild vinegar, such as rice or champagne vinegar, and lemon juice keeps the pucker within reason.

For us, a salad is incomplete without garlic. Mustard provides a better emulsion of oil and lemon, and it adds a little zip. For some people, garlic and mustard are really variations. It's up to you.

Start your vinaigrette in a large clean salad bowl (if it's wooden, be sure it's washed and sweet-smelling). First in is a dollop of Dijon mustard—1 rounded teaspoon is about right for 4 salad eaters—then a mashed and finely minced garlic clove. Add the lemon juice and/or vinegar, salt, and pepper and, beating with a whisk, drizzle in the oil. Taste for seasonings; adjustments are usually needed. The vinaigrette will improve if you make it ahead of time (no more than an hour) to let the flavors blend. Do not refrigerate it. Taste again before it goes on the greens.

How much dressing? Count on a tablespoon of oil for each large handful of greens (one serving) plus one for the bowl. Mix half the dressing with the greens and proceed cautiously from there.

We like our salads hand-tossed, literally. With surgically clean hands, toss the torn salad greens lightly but very, very well. Each leaf should end up with a glisten of dressing. Work rapidly so that the heat of your hands doesn't wilt the greens.

Tips:

Make the vinaigrette fresh for every salad. It develops an off-taste and separates stubbornly when kept in the refrigerator.

Shake the dressing together in a screw-top jar instead of mixing it in the salad bowl. This method is particularly good for salads with embellishments.

Use elegant, light dressings for soft and fluffy greens, gutsy dressings for heavier greens.

Variations:

Take 2 or 3 cloves of Roasted Garlic (page 151) and mix the pulp into a green herb or red pepper mustard.

Use a smoky mustard (wonderful on a mixed spinach salad) or a sweet and hot mustard for a heavier green salad.

Add snipped fresh herbs, such as dill, parsley, chervil, thyme, basil, mint.

Use lime juice instead of lemon and add grated orange zest and a lot of minced chives for a pleasing springlike taste. Great with grilled fish.

Add a finely diced shallot to the vinaigrette. Let it sit in the vinegar for half an hour to infuse the flavor before you finish making the dressing.

Whisk an egg yolk into a mustard-based vinaigrette (unless you're worried about salmonella, in which case skip the egg), then spike the flavor with a squirt of anchovy paste, minced scallions, and a dash or two of Worcestershire sauce. Use this dressing over crisp romaine and sprinkle grated Parmesan on top for an instant faux-Caesar salad.

Cream the vinaigrette with a tablespoon of heavy cream, as the French do. It whisks in beautifully and softens the vinegar edge.

Add yogurt to the vinaigrette; it takes the addition of crumbled blue cheese or Roquefort perfectly.

Experiment with flavored vinegars, such as raspberry, black currant, mint, tarragon, and other herbs. Fruit vinegars work well with nut oils, such as hazelnut, walnut, and almond. Use these oils sparingly because they are strongly scented and can overpower the light greens they suit best. Mix equal measures of nut oil and safflower oil, which has no flavor at all.

Main Dishes

SEAFOOD

Shrimp with Cashew Nuts

Shrimp in Chili Paste with Garlic

Shrimp Scorpio

Quick and Dirty Shrimp Curry

Thai-style Curry

Cape Scallops Sautéed with Garlic and
    Sun-dried Tomatoes

Portuguese Crab Cakes with Mint and Cilantro

Red Pepper Aioli

Salmon Slices with Walnut or Hazelnut
    Vinaigrette

Grilled Swordfish with Mustard

Baked Cod with Onions and Mint

Catfish Baked with Cheese

POULTRY

Chicken Broiled with Mustard, Herbs, and
    Bread Crumbs

Orange-spiced Chicken Wings

Garlicky Baked Chicken Pieces

Bangkok Chicken

Oven-fried Chicken

Braised Chicken Thighs with Spicy
   Tomato and Ginger Sauce
Great Roast Chicken
Spicy Sun-dried Tomato and Mushroom
   Roast Chicken
Asian Roast Chicken
Cornish Hens
Turkey
Rolled Stuffed Turkey Cutlets
Enchiladas Suizas

BEEF AND VEAL

Grilled Beef Tenderloin with Roquefort
   and Red Pepper Butter
Roquefort and Red Pepper Butter
Grilled Flank Steak on a Bed of
   Roasted Peppers and Onions
Spicy Skirt Steak with Cinnamon
Beef Braised in Coffee
Wild Mushroom Meat Loaf
Veal Scallops with Fennel
Veal Shanks

PORK

Roast Pork with Bay Leaves

Succulent Pork Roast with Fennel

Pork Slices with Prunes

Pork Tenderloin

James Beard's Braised Pork Chops

Microwave-braised Pork Chops

Stuffed Pork Chops

Sicilian Meatballs with Raisins and Pine
    Nuts

Ham Baked in Cola

Ham Steaks

Church-Supper Ham Loaf

LAMB

Roast Lamb with Monsieur Henny's Potato,
    Onion, and Tomato Gratin

Moghul Roasted Leg of Lamb

Yogurt Marinade

Rack of Lamb with Anise and Sweet Garlic

Lamb and Olive Balls

PASTA

Pasta with Gorgonzola
Pasta with Vodka
Pasta with Eggplant Sauce
Clams, Gremolata, and Linguine
Pasta with Crabmeat

*T*oday even the best of cooks complain about spending too much time and trouble cooking, unless, of course, it's being done for R & R. Even we have caught ourselves whining. We thought about this and concluded that it's not just the *time* in the kitchen we begrudge, it's having to *concentrate* on recipes and fuss with their complexities. With so much else competing for our attention, what we need is uncommonly good food prepared with minimal effort.

We all have a few fast recipes we can practically make in our sleep because we've cooked them so many times. In our attempts to expand our own repertoires, we've assembled a number of dishes that aren't all, strictly speaking, fast. Dinner won't necessarily be on the table in minutes because we are adamant about not sacrificing flavor. To achieve real flavor, you need either a brilliant combination of perfect ingredients tossed together quickly or a span of time that allows flavors to develop and interchange. The good news is that the flavoring time doesn't translate into active kitchen time for you. While some of our recipes are not literally quick, they are always simple. You can follow them with little thought or fuss, and it won't make much difference if your measurements aren't precise. The super-quick recipes, on the other hand, are real winners in the brilliant-combination category, and you need to measure carefully.

What are the secrets of developing flavor when you're cooking simply? First of all, you need the best ingredients—complex dishes can cover a multitude of imperfections, but simple cuisine requires good flavors and textures from the start. This generally means buying fresh, not frozen, fish and chicken from a high volume source; communicating with your butcher, if you can find one; seeking out the finest produce; sniffing your dried spices and herbs periodically to make sure they're still potent (Thanksgiving is a good time to replace them); stocking your kitchen with quality basic products; and keeping some culinary exotica on hand to spark up simple fare.

We've also included a series of tips from the experts on how to pack extra flavor into simple dishes—using dry marinades, for instance, or tucking seasoning paste under the skin of a roasting bird, or wrapping a slice of fish in foil with some savory tidbits to infuse it with flavor without adding any fat. Sometimes it's a question of knowing what to do with a particular cut of meat, which kind of crab to buy, or how to sweeten the taste of a very fishy fish.

We've assembled a collection of recipes we think will change the way you cook on an everyday basis and will encourage you to invite guests. In addition, we hope that our own recipes and variations will stimulate you to improvise. It's always been our experience that the very best meals are born out of sheer desperation, when there are only a few ingredients at hand and a limited number of possibilities for cooking them. It's then that your own creativity has to take over; if you refer back to the basic recipes for the essential tips, you'll be able to wing it and come up with some exciting combinations of your own. The secret of successful improvisation lies somewhere between your mind and your mouth. Think carefully about how the elements work together, check out the basic recipe procedures, and keep tasting.

Shrimp with Cashew Nuts

Ken Hom

Ken Hom calls this "fast food of great quality"—which exactly fits our criteria. It's a typical Hong Kong dish based on a classic Chinese cooking technique called "velveting." It is the perfect description for the way the surface of an ingredient looks and feels after it has been oil-blanched, a variation of the more familiar water-blanching. In Chinese cooking, oil-blanching acts as a flavor sealer and keeps various flavors separate. It also equalizes cooking times in a stir-fry of diverse ingredients.

SERVES 4 TO 6

Combine the shrimp with the coating ingredients in a medium bowl. Mix well and refrigerate for about 20 minutes.

Heat a wok or large skillet until it is hot and add the peanut oil. When the oil is just warm, quickly add the shrimp, stir to separate, and turn off the heat. Allow the shrimp to sit in the warm oil for about 2 minutes. Drain in a colander set inside a stainless steel bowl, retaining some of the oil.

Wipe the wok clean, return 1½ tablespoons of the drained oil to the wok, and add the ginger and scallions, stir-frying for 30 seconds. Stir in the cashew nuts and salt and continue to stir-fry for another 30 seconds. Return the shrimp to the wok with the remaining ingredients and stir-fry for another 2 minutes. Turn out on a platter and serve at once.

Serving Suggestion: Serve with vegetable fried rice (page 190).

1 pound medium shrimp, peeled and
   deveined

COATING

1 egg white
1 teaspoon salt
2 teaspoons cornstarch

½ cup peanut oil, for velveting
2 teaspoons finely chopped peeled
   fresh ginger
2 tablespoons finely chopped whole
   scallions
½ cup unsalted cashew nuts, roasted
½ teaspoon salt
1 tablespoon hoisin sauce
1 tablespoon rice wine
6 tablespoons chicken stock
½ teaspoon cornstarch mixed with
   ½ teaspoon water
1 teaspoon sesame oil

Variations:

Substitute chicken for shrimp.

From Barbara Tropp: Add minced garlic and hot-pepper flakes to the ginger and scallions, then plump the dish up with squares of sweet red peppers. Use either cashews or almonds.

EDITORS' KITCHEN

SHRIMP DISHES

There are hundreds of fast and simple shrimp dishes. Here are a few of our favorites.

SERVES 2

Shrimp in Chili Paste with Garlic

Peel and devein ½ pound (12 to 16) medium shrimp and sauté in a hot skillet or wok with 2 tablespoons vegetable oil until they are just firm to the touch (3 to 4 minutes). Remove the shrimp from the pan. Stir into the remaining oil 2 tablespoons of Chili Paste with Garlic (a Chinese condiment available in most supermarkets). Toss the shrimp back into the pan and coat lightly with the sauce. Cook for another minute. Sprinkle with minced fresh cilantro and serve with Coconut Rice (page 190).

SERVES 4

Shrimp Scorpio

Sauté 1 medium chopped onion over medium heat in 2 tablespoons *each* olive oil and butter along with 1 minced garlic clove, a dash of oregano, and ¼ teaspoon hot red-pepper flakes. Cook until soft but not brown. Remove from the pan and set aside. Drain a 28-ounce can of Italian plum tomatoes. Pull out the stem ends and tear the tomatoes into fat strips; set aside. Clean, wash, and dry 1 pound shrimp. Return the pan to the heat, add more butter and oil as needed, and sauté the shrimp until just pink and opaque. Do not cook through. Deglaze the pan with a jigger of ouzo (vodka will do). Reduce a bit and remove the pan from the heat.

Preheat the oven to 400°. In a large ovenproof baking dish, arrange shrimp in one layer, sprinkle with onion mixture, and place tomatoes on top. Cover the dish with crumbled feta and top with minced parsley and dill. Bake just until the cheese melts and the dish is hot throughout. This dish reheats well. Serve with buttered orzo, a green salad, and toasted pita bread to mop up the sauce.

SERVES 4

Quick and Dirty Shrimp Curry

Peel and devein 1 pound shrimp. Pat dry. Sauté 1 minced onion, 1 or 2 garlic cloves, and 1 tablespoon grated fresh ginger in 3 tablespoons clarified butter. Sauté the shrimp until just pink. Remove and reserve. Whisk in 1 tablespoon good-quality curry powder or paste and let it cook for 1 or 2 minutes without scorching. Add a squirt of tomato paste from a tube. Dust in just enough instant flour to soak up the excess butter. Whisk in well. Add enough hot chicken broth to make a generous, soupy sauce for the shrimp, which should now be added back to the sauce to reheat. Serve with basmati rice and a sprinkle of fresh minced cilantro, basil, or mint.

Thai-style Curry

Follow the directions for Quick and Dirty Shrimp Curry (above) with these changes: Sauté whole dried red chilies with the onion; omit the tomato paste and flour; substitute unsweetened coconut milk for half the broth; remove the chilies and add a few whole fresh basil leaves just before serving.

Cape Scallops Sautéed with Garlic and Sun-dried Tomatoes

Jasper White

Scallops are the ideal quick-cook dish. If you can find Nantucket cape scallops in your fish market (their season is winter), this is an inspired way to prepare them. The acidity of the sundried tomato is the perfect balance for the sweet cape scallop. Bay and sea scallops work well, too, of course.

1½ pounds cape scallops
Salt and freshly ground black pepper
3 tablespoons olive oil
2 tablespoons finely chopped garlic
1 cup julienned sun-dried tomatoes
Juice of ½ lemon
2 tablespoons unsalted butter
3 tablespoons chopped Italian parsley
Risotto or buttered pasta for serving

Pick through the scallops, removing the straps and any particles of shell. Place the scallops in a colander so that they are as dry as possible. Prepare, measure, and have all the ingredients ready to go. The cooking time for this dish is very short.

Heat the sauté pan (or pans) until smoking hot. Season the scallops with salt and pepper. Add the oil and then the scallops to the pan, leaving a little space for the garlic. As soon as the scallops hit the pan, add the garlic. Do not move the pan or stir the scallops.

After 30 seconds, add the sun-dried tomatoes and toss. Cook for 30 seconds more. Add the lemon juice, butter, and parsley. Remove from heat and toss or stir until butter melts. Check the seasoning. Serve immediately.

Serving Suggestions: Buttered angel hair pasta makes a nice base for the scallops. Or serve them over toasted rounds of Italian or French bread. A vegetable accompaniment never seems to work well with scallops; pack the vitamins into a salad instead.

Tips:

Since scallops very often throw off juice when they're sautéed, try this tip from Julia Child: Test one scallop by sautéing in a dry pan before starting to cook. If it exudes liquid, sauté the scallops separately, *very* briefly, to avoid watering down the sauce.

Use 2 pans if necessary to prevent overcrowding.

Cook scallops just before serving; they don't reheat well.

Be careful not to overcook scallops.

Steam or poach the tomatoes if they are completely dried; simply cut them into strips if they are packed in oil.

Portuguese Crab Cakes with Mint and Cilantro

(Bolinhos de Santola)

Joyce Goldstein

4 tablespoons unsalted butter

2 medium onions, finely minced
   (about 1¼ cups)

4 ribs celery, chopped

1 tablespoon dry mustard

1 teaspoon cayenne pepper

2 pounds crabmeat, picked over for
   cartilage

½ cup mayonnaise, preferably
   homemade

2 large eggs

¾ cup fresh bread crumbs

¼ cup chopped fresh mint leaves

¼ cup chopped cilantro

2 teaspoons grated lemon zest

Salt and freshly ground pepper to
   taste

1 cup dry bread crumbs

1 cup olive oil or as needed for frying

Red Pepper Aioli (recipe follows)

Unless you have a Portuguese grandmother, you've probably never had crab cakes like these. And your Portuguese grandmother hasn't either—Joyce Goldstein's version has a definite California style. The patties can be made a day ahead. To make this recipe really quick, use store-bought mayonnaise (see Tip) and canned red peppers (see Note).

SERVES 6 TO 8

Melt the butter in a medium saucepan over medium heat. Add the onions and celery; cook until translucent, 5 to 7 minutes. Add the dry mustard and cayenne; stir well and cook 3 more minutes. Let cool completely.

Add all the remaining ingredients except the dry bread crumbs, oil, and aioli to the onion mixture and combine well. Shape into 16 patties, about ½ inch thick. Coat each crab cake with dry bread crumbs. (At this point the cakes can be refrigerated on a baking sheet lined with baker's parchment or waxed paper up to 24 hours.)

Heat the olive oil in a large heavy skillet over medium-high heat. Add as many crab cakes as will fit without crowding and sauté until golden brown, about 3 minutes each side. Serve hot with red pepper aioli.

Char the peppers over an open flame or under the broiler until blackened on all sides. Transfer to a plastic container with a lid or a paper or plastic bag. Cover the container or close the bag and let the peppers steam for about 15 minutes. Peel the skins from the peppers, then cut the peppers in half, remove the stems, and scrape out the seeds. Puree the peppers in a blender or food processor.

To make the mayonnaise, whisk the egg yolks and half the lemon juice together in a mixing bowl or blend in a food processor. Gradually beat in the olive oil until a thick emulsion is attained. Set aside ½ cup for the *bolinhos*.

Add the pepper puree, garlic, and cayenne to the remaining mayonnaise. Season to taste with salt and add enough of the remaining lemon juice to bring up the red pepper flavor.

Serving Suggestions: Serve with sautéed mixed greens and James Beard's over-baked potatoes (page 164) to sop up the extra aioli.

Tip: To make store-bought mayonnaise taste a bit more like homemade, whisk an egg yolk in a small, deep bowl and add a healthy squeeze or two of fresh lemon juice; whisk in 1 cup bottled mayonnaise, ¼ cup at a time. (If you are concerned about salmonella, use only commercial mayonnaise.)

Variations: Substitute for the raw pureed garlic a puree of Roasted Garlic (page 151) or of peeled garlic cloves that have been zapped, covered, in the microwave with a little oil until soft enough to puree.

Red Pepper Aioli

2 medium red peppers

MAYONNAISE

2 large egg yolks, at room temperature
2 tablespoons fresh lemon juice
2 cups mild olive oil

1 tablespoon smooth pureed garlic
½ teaspoon cayenne pepper, or to taste
Salt to taste

Note: Use lump or backfin crab or the less expensive cartilage-free claw meat (sweet despite its pale gray color and small pieces). Also look for pasteurized crab meat in the fish section of your supermarket. The quality is excellent, and the extended keeping time for an unopened tin makes crabmeat more practical to have at hand.

Use roasted peppers from a can or jar instead of roasting your own; look for the Mancini label.

Salmon Slices with Walnut or Hazelnut Vinaigrette

(Tranches de saumon tièdes à la vinaigrette de noix ou de noisettes)

Madeleine Kamman

We thought this recipe sounded almost too simple to be memorable, but we were wrong—this is an elegant, aromatic, and delicious way to serve salmon.

*B*rush the skillet with 1 tablespoon of the oil. Heat it well. Sear the salmon pieces on one side. Turn over, season with salt and pepper, and sear on the second side. Cover and let the fish cook in the hot pan, in its own juices and off the heat, for 6 to 8 minutes. Remove to a dish.

To the skillet add the remaining 6 tablespoons of the oil. Squeeze the shallots in the corner of a towel and add them. Add the walnuts or hazelnuts, depending on which oil you have used, the vinegar, and salt and pepper. Whisk well to homogenize and pour evenly over the pieces of fish. Sprinkle with parsley. Serve lukewarm or marinate overnight to serve cold the next day.

Serving Suggestions: Serve with Skillet Scallions (page 178) and Potato Gratin (page 172).

Tip: Have the fishmonger remove the bones from the salmon steaks.

Variations:
Use avocado or safflower oil instead of nut oil.

Cook the salmon and sauce *en papillote,* a foil or parchment package. Enfold the salmon and sauce in the package and plunk it in a preheated 375° oven for 10 to 12 minutes. Here are some other good flavor combinations for salmon *en papillote:*

- Mix 1 tablespoon orange juice concentrate with 1 teaspoon lemon juice and ¼ cup heavy cream. Pour over the fish, and for each serving add 1 teaspoon finely minced garlic, chives, and parsley mixed with finely grated orange zest.

7 tablespoons walnut or hazelnut oil
6 salmon medaillions, ¾ inch thick
Salt
Pepper from the mill
2 shallots, chopped very fine
2 tablespoons finely chopped walnuts
    or chopped toasted hazelnuts
1½ tablespoons balsamic vinegar or
    1 tablespoon sherry mixed with
    ½ tablespoon cider vinegar
2 tablespoons chopped parsley

- Drizzle the fish with dry white wine and top each piece with a thin lemon slice, a thin pat of butter, and a lot of chopped fresh dill.

- Make a sauce of 1 tablespoon dry sherry, ¼ cup light soy sauce, 1 pressed garlic clove, 1 teaspoon finely slivered fresh ginger, and a few splashes of dark sesame oil, and pour over the fish.

Grilled Swordfish with Mustard

Susan Feniger and Mary Sue Milliken

5 tablespoons Dijon mustard
2 tablespoons olive oil
6 tablespoons clam juice
½ cup minced shallots
½ cup chopped fresh chives
½ teaspoon white pepper
6 (7-ounce) swordfish fillets
Salt and white pepper to taste
Olive oil for brushing

This entire dish can be put together in ten minutes, so it's perfect for last-minute entertaining.

SERVES 6

Preheat grill as hot as possible.

Mix mustard, olive oil, clam juice, shallots, chives, and pepper in a small bowl. Cover with plastic wrap and reserve.

Season fish all over with salt and pepper. Grill about 3 minutes per side, brushing with olive oil after turning. Transfer onto serving plates, spoon sauce over grilled fish, and serve immediately.

Serving Suggestions: Serve with grilled zucchini, onions, thick red pepper strips, and Spiced Masa Muffins (page 205).

Tips:
From Paula Wolfert: Rub swordfish steaks well with a mixture of 6 parts olive oil and 1 part lemon juice, in addition to salt and pepper, before grilling.

Feniger and Milliken offer a great oven-roasting alternative to grilling fish: Sear the fillets in a skillet with an ovenproof handle in 4 tablespoons butter for 1 minute on each side. Finish the cooking in a preheated 450° oven for 3 to 5 minutes.

Variations:

Serve with brown butter or, better still, brown butter with puree of Roasted Garlic (page 151). For 6 servings, heat 4 tablespoons unsalted butter over medium-high heat until it turns golden brown. Don't let it burn. Whisk 2 tablespoons of the hot butter into ¼ cup roasted garlic puree, then add back into the butter. Serve at once.

Marinate the fish in curried yogurt for at least 1 hour before grilling (for 6 servings, whisk 1 tablespoon good-quality curry powder or paste into 1½ cups yogurt). Serve with Spinach Pilaf (page 192).

Baked Cod with Onions and Mint

(Merluzzo all'istriana)

Joyce Goldstein

Like catfish away from the South, cod outside New England has a poor image. As Joyce Goldstein says, "It isn't glamorous enough." Try her simple recipe from the Italian province of Friuli to taste what you've been missing.

6 tablespoons unsalted butter
3 medium onions, sliced ¼ inch thick
2 garlic cloves, finely minced
1 cup finely chopped fresh mint leaves
1 cup finely chopped fresh flat-leaf
    parsley
Salt and freshly ground pepper
4 cod fillets, 6 to 7 ounces each
2 tablespoons olive oil
2 tablespoons fresh lemon juice
2 green onions, chopped
2 tablespoons capers, rinsed well
4 anchovies, rinsed, cut into long
    strips

SERVES 4

*P*reheat the oven to 450°. Melt the butter in a medium saucepan over medium heat. Add the onions and cook until tender. Add the garlic and cook a minute or two, then add the mint and parsley and cook a minute longer. Season to taste with salt and pepper.

Spread the onion mixture in a shallow baking pan just large enough to hold the cod. Arrange the cod fillets on top and brush them with olive oil and lemon juice. Sprinkle with salt and pepper.

Bake until cooked through but still juicy, about 10 minutes. Transfer the fish and onion mixture to serving plates. Garnish with the green onions, capers, and anchovies.

Serving Suggestions: Serve with Baked Red Beets (page 136) or Braised Garlic and String Beans (page 153) and Steamed Rice (page 189).

Tips:
Fish cooked in the microwave comes out spectacularly well. Cook 6- to 8-ounce fillets in 2 to 5 minutes,

depending on the number of pieces and the wattage of your oven. Use just a little liquid to flavor the fish, if you like, or none at all; in fact, it tends to slow cooking time because fish cooks faster than it takes water to boil.

Compensate for the dry heat when baking fish in the oven by using a braising liquid, a coating, or a wrapper (parchment or foil). Or use the oven-roasting method described on page 59.

Braise cod in milk. It keeps that lovely white flesh white and erases even the slightest fishy taste.

You can time fish by the Canadian method—10 minutes to the inch at the thickest part—or cook it until it flakes, though some critics contend the fish is overdone by then. Or cook it to an internal temperature of 145°—but it's hard for us to imagine poking a thermometer into fish, even if aficionados do. The test we rely on is Julia Child's: It is done "when you begin to smell the buttery aroma of cooking fish and you notice that juices are just beginning to appear in the platter." Whichever method you choose, be sure the fish has lost its translucency and the flesh has just begun to firm up; if not, return it to the heat for a minute.

Catfish Baked with Cheese

Craig Claiborne

6 catfish fillets (about 2 pounds)
½ cup freshly grated Parmesan
¼ cup flour
Salt to taste, if desired
Freshly ground black pepper to taste
1 teaspoon paprika
1 egg, lightly beaten
1 tablespoon milk
8 tablespoons (1 stick) butter, melted
¼ cup sliced almonds

One would think a fish called cat would inspire a lot more enthusiasm than catfish does. This sweet, mild, utterly delicious fish has a lot going for it—and this recipe is a perfect example.

SERVES 6

Preheat the oven to 350°. Wipe the catfish dry.

Blend together the Parmesan, flour, salt, pepper, and paprika. Combine the egg and milk in a flat dish.

Dip the fillets in the egg mixture and then coat with the cheese mixture. Arrange the fillets in one layer in a baking dish, and pour the butter over. Sprinkle with the almonds and place in the oven and bake for 20 minutes.

Serving Suggestions: Serve with Peas and Cucumber in Dill (page 162) or Asparagus Poêlé (page 134).

Tips:
Don't be tempted to pan-fry these; the Parmesan cheese would tend to burn on the direct heat of the skillet.

Remove head of catfish, but leave on tail; it retains moisture in the fish, and it's deliciously crispy.

Variation: Cut the fish into little strips or *goujonettes.* First cut the fillets in half, then slice them on the diagonal into ½-inch strips. Dip the strips in milk (or let them soak for 15 minutes or so), then in fine cornmeal seasoned with salt, pepper, and cayenne. Fry in hot peanut oil for 2 to 3 minutes. Be sure not to crowd the strips in the pan. Drain on paper towels and keep warm in the oven. Serve with a dipping sauce of hot mustard or minced jalapeños whisked into mayonnaise. *Goujonettes* also make a good starter.

Mustard and chicken are a classic combination. Here the mustard seasoning coats the outside of the chicken to give it a savory crisp skin. It's a great make-ahead dish that is delicious cold or at room temperature.

Chicken Broiled with Mustard, Herbs, and Bread Crumbs

(Poulets grillés à la diable)

Julia Child

SERVES 4 TO 8

𝒫reheat oven broiler to moderately hot.

Dry the chicken thoroughly. Combine the melted butter and oil and paint the chicken with it. Arrange the chicken skin side down in the bottom of the broiling pan. Place it so that the surface of the chicken is 5 to 6 inches from the hot broiling element and broil 10 minutes on each side, basting every 5 minutes. The chicken should be very lightly browned. Salt it lightly.

Blend the mustard with the shallots or onions, herbs, and seasonings in a bowl. Drop by drop, beat in half the basting fat to make a mayonnaiselike cream. Reserve the rest of the basting fat for later. Paint the chicken pieces with the mustard mixture.

Pour the crumbs on a big plate, then roll chicken in the crumbs, patting them on so they adhere.

Arrange the chicken pieces skin side down on the rack in the broiling pan and dribble half the remaining basting fat over them. Brown slowly for 10 minutes under a moderately hot broiler. Turn, baste with the last of the fat, and brown 10 minutes more on the other side. The chicken is done when the thickest part of the drumstick is tender and the juices run clear yellow when the meat is pricked with a fork.

2 ready-to-cook, 2½-pound broilers, halved or quartered

6 tablespoons melted butter

2 tablespoons oil

Salt

6 tablespoons prepared mustard of the strong Dijon type

3 tablespoons finely minced shallots or green onions

½ teaspoon thyme, basil, or tarragon

⅛ teaspoon pepper

Pinch of cayenne pepper

4 cups fresh white bread crumbs (make the crumbs in an electric blender, 3 or 4 slices of bread at a time)

Serving Suggestions: Serve with Broccoli Smothered in Garlic Oil (page 138) and steamed basmati rice (page 189).

Tips:

The success of this dish depends on having the crumbs just dry enough to form a crisp coating. Leave the bread you plan to use uncovered overnight; don't fan it out on the counter, just allow the air to get at it. Bakery bread makes the best crumbs.

Coat the chicken ahead of time, leave it, uncovered, in the refrigerator overnight, and just finish it off in the oven.

Orange-spiced Chicken Wings

Ken Haedrich

If you're unfamiliar with chicken wings, this subtle preparation will be a real treat. There isn't much meat even on the bigger wings, but it's the sweetest meat on the whole chicken. This is a good do-ahead dish for a casual supper and would be perfect in tandem with a baked ham on a company buffet table.

SERVES 4

1½ cups buttermilk
⅓ cup maple syrup
2 oranges, halved and sections cut out
1 teaspoon cinnamon
16 to 20 chicken wings

$\mathcal{M}$ix the buttermilk and maple syrup in a large bowl. Briefly process the orange sections and cinnamon in a blender to make a coarse puree. Stir the orange mixture into the buttermilk, then add the chicken wings. Stir to coat. Cover and refrigerate for at least 1 hour or up to 24 hours, stirring every now and then. Grill or broil, far enough from the heat to prevent excessive charring.

Turn from time to time, brushing with some of the buttermilk marinade.

Serving Suggestions: Serve with Corn Fritters (page
145) and Stir-fried Zucchini with Sesame Seeds (page
184).

Tips:

Add a couple of spoonfuls of orange juice concentrate
to the orange puree or finely grate the zest before cutting out the sections and stir it into the marinade to
intensify the orange flavor.

Buy the plumpest, meatiest chicken wings you can find.
Chop off the wing tips and freeze them to toss into the
stockpot. Cut the remaining hinged wing in half at the
joint with a quick stroke of a sharp cleaver.

Variations:

Substitute another marinade; virtually any one that
works for a whole chicken or chicken parts works for
wings. You can also use a commercial barbecue sauce;
taste it and see if it would benefit from a little garlic,
cayenne, or lemon juice.

For an Asian version, mix 4 crushed garlic cloves and 1
tablespoon minced fresh ginger with ¾ cup soy sauce.
Add 1 tablespoon Chinese hot chili paste and 2 tablespoons rice wine vinegar, dry sherry, or lemon juice.
Marinate the wings overnight or at least 2 hours. For a
high gloss, brush the wings with honey during the last 5
or 10 minutes of grilling or broiling. Serve with shrimp
or pork fried rice (page 191).

Garlicky Baked Chicken Pieces

This is one of our favorite dinners along with a big salad. It's worth cooking the dish just for the kitchen aroma.

SERVES 4

Marinate 8 chicken thighs or whole legs for at least 1 hour in a mixture of ½ cup olive oil, 4 crushed garlic cloves, dried oregano to taste, lots of freshly ground black pepper, and the juice of 1 lemon. Preheat the oven to 500°. Bake the chicken for 15 minutes, turn it over, and bake for 10 to 15 minutes more. Drain on paper towels and serve hot or at room temperature.

Bangkok Chicken

Hugh Carpenter and Teri Sandison

1 3-pound chicken, cut into pieces
Freshly ground black pepper
3 tablespoons butter, cut into pieces
1 tablespoon cornstarch

This recipe is the epitome of carefree cuisine—easy, exotic, and very appealing for a company dinner. This is not a searingly hot Thai dish, and that flavor element can always be controlled by adjusting the amount of chili sauce.

SERVES 4

Preheat oven to 425°.

Place chicken in a roasting pan and season with pepper. Dot chicken with butter, then roast for about 30 to 40 minutes, basting every 10 minutes with pan juices. Chicken is done when internal temperature reaches 165° on a meat thermometer and when the juices run clear.

While the chicken roasts, combine cornstarch with an equal amount of cold water. Combine garlic, ginger, green onions, basil, and mint in a separate bowl. Combine remaining sauce ingredients. Set aside.

When the chicken is cooked, remove it from the roasting pan. Discard all but 2 tablespoons fat from pan, then place pan over high heat and add garlic mixture. Bring to a low boil, scraping up pan drippings, and stir in a little cornstarch mixture to lightly thicken sauce. Taste sauce and adjust seasonings. Return chicken to pan and coat evenly with sauce. Place chicken on heated dinner plates and garnish with mint sprigs. Serve at once.

Serving Suggestions: Serve as an entree with vegetable fried rice (page 191) or rice noodles. For a company buffet, partner the chicken with a platter of Shrimp in Chili Paste with Garlic (page 50) and a salad of ripe tropical fruits with a lime vinaigrette.

Note: Unsweetened Thai coconut milk is available in the gourmet section of some supermarkets. Don't substitute sweetened coconut milk which is best for mixed drinks.

Variation: Make the sauce separately to serve over charcoal-grilled chicken or lamb or jumbo shrimp. It can be made well ahead of time and reheated in the microwave. Use 2 tablespoons butter instead of chicken drippings to sauté the garlic and onions.

SAUCE

3 garlic cloves, finely minced
1 tablespoon finely minced fresh ginger
¼ cup minced green onions
¼ cup minced fresh basil
2 tablespoons minced fresh mint
1 cup unsweetened coconut milk
2 tablespoons light soy sauce
½ teaspoon turmeric
½ teaspoon Chinese chili sauce
¼ teaspoon salt
Mint sprigs, for garnish

Oven-fried Chicken

Marcia Adams

⅓ cup vegetable oil
⅓ cup (⅔ stick) butter
1 cup all-purpose flour
1 teaspoon salt
2 teaspoons black pepper
2 teaspoons paprika
1 teaspoon garlic salt
1 teaspoon dried marjoram (optional)
8 to 9 chicken pieces, legs, thighs,
    breasts

Most oven-fried chicken is dreadful, not at all like the real thing, but here's an exception: This chicken is moist, crisp, and succulent. You can cut the amount of butter in half and the chicken will still be delicious.

SERVES 4 TO 5

Place the oil and butter in a shallow cooking pan (a jelly-roll pan is perfect) and put in a preheated 375° oven to melt. Set aside.

In a large paper sack, combine the flour and seasonings. Roll the chicken pieces, 3 at a time, in the melted oil-butter mixture, then drop them in the sack and shake to cover. Place on a dish or wax paper.

Place chicken in the pan, skin side down. Bake for 45 minutes. With a spatula, turn over and bake 5 to 10 minutes longer, or until the top crust begins to bubble. Serve hot or cold, but the crust texture is better if chicken is not refrigerated before eating. If you can afford the calories, the pan drippings make an absolutely divine gravy for either mashed potatoes or baking powder biscuits.

Serving Suggestions: Serve with Big Baked Onions (page 158) and Early Summer Fresh Corn Pudding (page 146) or Mashed Potatoes (page 166).

Tips:
Check the chicken to be sure it's done. We like this dish best with chicken thighs, which take a few minutes longer.

We think garlic powder is preferable to garlic salt.

Variations:

Try this procedure with chicken wings; they're great for cocktails.

Use Cajun chicken seasoning instead of garlic salt or powder for a spicy version.

Add a little ground allspice.

Braised Chicken Thighs with Spicy Tomato and Ginger Sauce

Ken Hom

1 tablespoon peanut oil

1½ pounds (about 6) chicken thighs

Salt and freshly ground black pepper
   to taste

1 can (28 ounces) peeled tomatoes
   without juice, coarsely chopped in
   a food processor or food mill

2 tablespoons finely chopped garlic

1 tablespoon finely chopped fresh
   ginger

1 small fresh hot chili, chopped

2 teaspoons sugar

½ cup fresh coriander, loosely packed

This dish features an assertive sauce with the unique accent of ginger. Chicken thighs hold up very well to this sauce, better than breasts or wings. The dish reheats perfectly and tastes even better the next day.

SERVES 2 TO 4

In a medium frying pan, heat the peanut oil over moderate heat. Brown the thighs on both sides, beginning with the skin side. Salt and pepper them while browning the second side. Drain the thighs on paper towels and set aside.

Drain the fat from the frying pan except for 2 teaspoons. Add the tomatoes, garlic, ginger, chili, and sugar, and cook over moderately high heat for about 8 minutes. Reduce to a low simmer.

Return the thighs to the skillet, cover, and braise slowly for 20 minutes. Add the coriander at the very end of the cooking.

Serving Suggestions: Serve with Corn Fritters (page 145) and a flat-leaf spinach salad or a basmati rice pilaf (page 189) and steamed broccoli florets.

Tips:
If you can't find fresh chilies—which always seem plentiful when you don't need them—use hot red-pepper flakes or canned jalapeño, rinsed, stemmed, and seeded.

Use boneless chicken thighs, cut in half; they take a little less time to cook.

EDITORS' KITCHEN

There are some dishes everyone prepares successfully without thought or hesitation. You've done them over and over, and it's those dishes that give you your culinary confidence. One of them is undoubtedly your famous roast chicken. Now we come along to suggest that we can all afford to rethink how to roast a chicken—and we're a bit chagrined to admit we've shaped up our own skills in the process.

We've tried many ways of roasting chicken: in buttered paper bags; at very low temperatures, at high temperatures, at varying temperatures; stuffed, unstuffed; trussed, not trussed; breast up, breast down; sideways and every subtlety between. This is what we've learned:

• A broad-breasted four- to six-pound roasting chicken is best. Small birds (broilers and fryers) tend to be flavorless and don't roast successfully. They dry out in a hot oven, and they always require marinating and basting for flavor. A stunning exception to this rule is Marcella Hazan's famous self-basting lemon roast chicken which requires a smaller (2½-pound) bird. Soften 2 lemons in the microwave for 15 seconds, then pierce them all over many times with a fork. Salt and pepper the chicken thoroughly, inside and out, then insert the lemons into the cavity of the chicken. Roast the chicken, breast down, at 350° for 15 minutes, breast up for another 20 minutes. A final 15 minutes at 400° (breast still up) and the chicken is done.

• The bird will cook faster and more evenly if it isn't stuffed or trussed. Just be warned that it will look less elegant on the platter with legs and wings akimbo.

Great Roast Chicken

- An adjustable rack will cradle the bird in the roasting pan and allow you to cook it breast down, which, for the high-temperature method, helps retain moisture in the breast meat. But if you don't have a rack, rest the bird on some crumpled aluminum foil or just put it directly in the pan.

- A little extra flavoring should be tucked into the rinsed and dried cavity of an unstuffed bird: a few peeled garlic cloves; half a lemon, lime, or orange; a quartered onion; a piece of bread fried in butter and rubbed with garlic; a few sprigs of herbs; and, always, salt and pepper. Salt and pepper the chicken all over just before you put it in the oven.

- For the crispiest skin, leave the chicken, uncovered, on a sheet of foil in the refrigerator the night before roasting. The skin will become dry and taut.

Whether to roast a five-pound bird at 500° for 50 minutes or at 375° for 75 minutes—that is the question. We prefer the high temperature, at the cost of a messy oven. The chicken will have crisp skin and juicy meat, and you will save a good 25 minutes. Let the chicken rest for 10 minutes, tail up, says French chef Joel Robuchon, to remoisten the breast before carving. You may want to salt and pepper the chicken again before slicing it. (To save cleaning up a messy oven, cover the bottom of the roasting pan with coarse salt to catch the drippings before they smoke.)

SEASONING UNDER THE SKIN

This is one of the best ways to build flavor into a roast chicken or a turkey. It not only flavors the meat, but if you're using the hot-oven method, it protects the breast meat from drying out. What you do is make a compound butter or seasoning paste (see below) and spread it under the skin onto the meat of the chicken. This is easier to do than it sounds. (Compound butters and seasoning pastes can also be used under the skin of a whole chicken or turkey breast or Cornish hens.)

To spread seasoning under the skin of a bird, loosen the skin from the breast and wiggle your fingers in over the meat. If you're careful, you can actually get your whole hand in. The easiest way to get the butter or paste on the chicken flesh is to put a dab on your closed fingers and smear it directly over the meat. You don't need more than a very thin coverage. Lifting the skin of the legs is a bit trickier, so be careful not to tear it.

Compound Butters

To make a compound butter, process (or mash with a fork) a stick of unsalted butter until soft, then process with flavorings to taste. Roll the butter in a piece of aluminum foil and refrigerate until ready to use. Freeze for longer storage. Here's a partial list of compound butters and pastes you can use for poultry and other dishes. Before long, you'll be adding your own concoctions to the list. Be sure to bring the butters to room temperature before spreading.

- Citrus Butter (grated lemon, lime, or orange zest)

- Curry and Orange Butter (curry powder and orange zest with pressed garlic)

- Herb Butter (fresh or dried herbs)

- Cilantro Butter (chopped cilantro with a squeeze of lemon)

- Spicy Butter (cayenne, hot-pepper flakes, or chili paste)

- Chili Butter (commercial chili powder)

- Roasted-Garlic Butter (see page 151 for Roasted Garlic)

- Green or Black Olive Paste (in tubes or jars)

- Pesto (thinned out with olive oil and with more garlic added)

MARINADES

Chicken can be marinated at room temperature for at least two hours or in the refrigerator for up to forty-eight hours. Longer marinating heightens flavor. The marinade can be either wet or dry. If you don't have time, switch to under-the-skin seasoning.

Dry Marinade

A blend of fresh or dried herbs and spices can be rubbed into the skin along with salt and pepper. For example:

- Rosemary and thyme

- Chinese five-spice powder

- Cajun seasonings such as Paul Prudhomme's

- Chili powder, cumin, and red pepper

You can make a dry marinade into a paste by adding oil and pressed garlic, even tomato or anchovy paste. Paste marinades are easier to spread, but remember to dry the skin well so the paste marinade will stick.

Wet Marinade

A wine-, citrus-, or yogurt-based mixture will tender-
ize the meat as well as flavor it. For example:

- Three parts olive oil to one part red wine together
  with minced garlic and onion, dried herbs, salt, and
  pepper

- One cup yogurt mixed with one tablespoon tandoori
  or curry powder; mix the curry powder with a little
  oil and heat gently to release the flavor.

- Commercially bottled marinade or barbecue sauce

- Undiluted orange or tangerine concentrate, soy sauce,
  and honey

- Lemon juice, grated lemon zest, and fresh mint or
  tarragon

Put the chicken and the wet marinade in a plastic bag
with a twist or zip lock. Squish the marinade around the
bird and store in the refrigerator; turn the bag over once
in a while to assure good coverage.

PAN SAUCES

If you've seasoned the chicken well and roasted it at a
moderate temperature, you will have the most delicious
pan juices to start a sauce.

To make a pan sauce, pour off most of the fat or remove
it with a bulb baster. While the chicken is resting, put
the roasting pan over the largest burner (or two) and
bring the juices to a simmer. Blot up the remaining surface fat with a few shakes of instant flour and whisk

well. (If you want to intensify the seasonings you've already used, add more to the pan before thickening.) Now choose a compatible liquid—chicken broth, wine, fruit juice concentrate, coffee, Madeira, port, and/or light cream. Whisk in about 1 cup of liquid, allowing the flour to lightly thicken the sauce. Taste and adjust the seasoning.

Here are a couple of ideas to start you off on your own improvisations.

Spicy Sun-dried Tomato and Mushroom Roast Chicken

Make an under-the-skin mixture of 2 tablespoons tomato paste (or sun-dried tomato paste from a tube), 6 finely slivered sun-dried tomatoes, 4 pressed or minced garlic cloves, 2 or 3 rinsed anchovy fillets, hot red-pepper flakes to taste, and just enough olive oil to make it spreadable. Spread this mixture under the skin of the chicken, then run your paste-covered fingers over the outside of the bird. Put a few fresh herb sprigs in the cavity. Roast the chicken as described on pages 71 and 72 until done. Set aside while you make the sauce.

Add 2 cups sliced cremini mushrooms to the hot pan drippings and toss rapidly over high heat until they are flecked with golden brown. Stirring rapidly, drizzle in enough dry red wine to emulsify the pan juices; cook for a couple of minutes, just long enough to burn off the alcohol. If you like, add a touch more tomato paste or some heavy cream to thicken and enrich the sauce. Add a small handful of chopped fresh herbs or minced parsley and salt and pepper to taste. Serve this sauce over the pieces of chicken or over an accompaniment of sautéed polenta (page 195).

Asian Roast Chicken

Make a wet marinade of ¼ cup dark soy sauce, ¼ cup hoisin sauce, 2 tablespoons light sesame oil, 2 tablespoons peanut oil, 1 tablespoon Chinese or Thai chili sauce, 3 minced garlic cloves, and 1 tablespoon minced fresh ginger. Place the chicken in a plastic bag, pour in the marinade, and squish it around. Seal the bag and refrigerate for 2 hours, turning once or twice. Roast the chicken as described on pages 71 and 72 until done. Remove from the oven and let rest while you make the sauce.

Pour off most of the chicken fat from the roasting pan and add 2 minced garlic cloves, 6 slivered scallions, and 1 tablespoon chopped cilantro. Slowly add 1 cup hot chicken stock to the pan, scraping up all the drippings and bits of chicken. Mix 1 tablespoon cornstarch and 1 tablespoon sherry and use this to thicken the sauce. Serve the sauce over the pieces of chicken. Accompany with vegetable fried rice (page 191).

Cornish Hens

Chickens are about as beloved in America as Mickey Mouse, but Cornish hens are another story. We think it's because way back when—when Victor Borge introduced them—they were smaller, less meaty, and not worth the hill of bones left on the plate. But now they are little hens of substance. We find Cornish hens sweeter than chickens (they are all white meat) and easier and faster to cook. A 1½-pound hen is perfect for two people, without leftovers. We prefer to split the hen—the compact portion looks attractive, cooks faster, and is easier to eat.

To split a Cornish hen, cut through the bones—they are very soft—with a cleaver, sharp knife, or poultry shears. Cut the bird down one side of the backbone, lay it out flat on a cutting board, and whack off the backbone and tail. With the flat side of a cleaver or large knife, flatten the hen at the breastbone by hitting the cleaver with the side of your fist a couple of times. Or remove the breastbone altogether, which is easier to do than you might think. At first you'll wonder what to do with the leg and wing, but logic will show you how to make it look like half a bird again. It does not have to be trussed to hold its shape.

Split birds can be marinated, seasoned under the skin, or roasted plain. Our favorite method is to pre-cook the bird in the microwave, then finish it under the broiler or on the grill. The hens come out moist and juicy and well infused with the seasoning.

To cook a split Cornish hen, season or marinate the bird, cover it tightly, and precook both halves at full power in the microwave for about 6 minutes (about 10 minutes for a whole bird). Baste with the pan juices, which should be saved for sauce (page 75). Put the bird under a preheated broiler for 5 minutes on each side, or just long enough to crisp the skin and cook the meat through. Use the same method if you choose to finish the cooking on the outdoor grill.

You can also roast whole Cornish hens at 375° about 45 minutes for a one-pounder; be careful not to over-cook them because they dry out easily. The hot-oven method is not recommended for these tender little birds.

Turkey

The big bird has trotted right into star status as health consciousness spotlights its many virtues. Holiday turkey is unbeatable, of course, but we also love cold turkey, especially in summer. When turkey's at its best, it's moist and subtly delicious. The best insurance is to buy a fresh turkey or a deep-chilled one from a reliable producer. Ignore the prebasted turkeys entirely.

Roasting turkey at a high temperature may seem like a good idea, and it is—it produces a crisp skin and moist meat—but you also run the risk of undercooking the dark meat. To

minimize the risk, don't truss the turkey so the hot air can cir-
culate all around the dark meat.

Barbara Kafka is the woman who brought America hot-
roasted turkey, and here's her advice: Have the bird at room
temperature. Put the oven rack at the lowest level and raise the
heat to 500°. You do not need a pan rack; just slide the turkey
in its pan, legs first, into the hot oven. After 15 minutes, slide
it around (using a wooden spatula) to keep it from sticking; do
this every 20 minutes. If it seems to be getting too dark, cover
it with foil. Roast till the thigh joint moves easily; the bird will
be done in about 10 minutes.

Cooking time is almost too good to be true. A 10-pound
turkey takes 75 minutes, a 12-pounder just 5 minutes more, a
15-pounder just under two hours. If the turkey's stuffed, add
another half hour to the time.

Remove the turkey to a serving platter, cover with a foil
tent, and set aside to rest—tail up—for about twenty minutes
before carving.

TURKEY BREAST ROAST

If the delights of roast turkey with stuffing aren't on the
agenda, consider a turkey breast roast. Because the
breast needs to cook only to 160° to be perfectly done
(while the dark meat should be 180° or 185°), a turkey
breast roast will cook in a matter of minutes, not hours.

To cook a turkey breast roast, self-baste it by seasoning
it under the skin with a compound butter (page 73) or
by tucking it into a new brown paper bag with no let-
tering on it and smearing the inside of the bag with
softened butter. Place the roast in a standard roasting pan
(no rack required), breast up, and cook at 350° for 15

to 20 minutes per pound, or to an internal temperature of 160°.

Turkey breast is also a natural for microwave cooking, since moisture retention is important for its success. Check your oven's instruction booklet for the correct time.

TURKEY LEGS

Some people love drumsticks, but we don't like those corset stays and prefer just to add the legs to the soup pot. The thighs, however, are delicious eating—try them with the sauce for Spicy Skirt Steak with Cinnamon (page 89): Bake them at 350° until the internal temperature reaches 185°, or until the meat falls away from the bone.

TURKEY SOUP

The leftover carcass from a roast turkey makes a wonderful soup.

To make turkey soup, take the meat off the bones as soon as dinner is over and toss the carcass into a big pot with a large carrot, a quartered onion, a couple of celery ribs, several garlic cloves, some peppercorns, a bay leaf, and salt. Add the wing tips and neck. Cover with water, bring to a boil, and simmer for a couple of hours, skimming occasionally. Let the soup cool, remove the large bones, and strain the rest. Season to taste, add some cooked white or wild rice, and your soup is ready and waiting.

These turkey rolls remind us of veal birds, an old favorite that now rarely appears on the best-dressed tables. Turkey cutlets can easily become dried out and tasteless, but these savory little rolls are moist and lively.

Rolled Stuffed Turkey Cutlets

(Involtini di tacchino)

Giuliano Bugialli

SERVES 6

6 ½-inch-thick turkey cutlets, sliced from the breast
6 sweet Italian sausages, without fennel seeds, or 18 ounces ground pork
6 large sage leaves, fresh or preserved in salt
1 medium garlic clove, peeled
2 tablespoons rosemary leaves, fresh or preserved in salt or dried and blanched
4 tablespoons olive oil
2 tablespoons unsalted butter
1 cup dry white wine
1 cup canned imported Italian tomatoes, drained
Salt and freshly ground black pepper
15 sprigs of Italian parsley, leaves only
About 30 large black Greek olives in brine, drained

Pound the cutlets between two pieces of wax paper that have been dampened with cold water so the meat does not stick to the paper.

Lay out the pounded cutlets on a board and place a sausage on each one. Wrap the turkey cutlets around the sausages and tie these *involtini* like small salamis.

Finely chop the sage, garlic, and rosemary together on a board.

Heat the oil and butter in a casserole, preferably of terra cotta or enamel, over medium heat. When the butter is completely melted, add the chopped ingredients and sauté for 2 minutes. Put in the *involtini* and sauté for 5 minutes, turning them many times in order to cook them evenly, but keeping them very light in color.

Add the wine and let it evaporate for 15 minutes.

Pass the tomatoes through a food mill, using the disc with the small holes, into the casserole. Season with salt and pepper and cook, covered, for 20 minutes longer.

Meanwhile, coarsely chop the parsley on a board.

Add the olives to the casserole and mix very well. Then add the parsley and cook for 10 minutes longer.

Remove the string from the *involtini* and transfer the contents of the casserole to a warmed platter. Serve immediately.

Serving Suggestions: Serve with Cauliflower with Raisins and Pine Nuts (page 142) or Pureed Celery Root with Apples (page 144). Start with one of the skillet pastas (pages 27–28).

Tip: To tie the meat "like a salami" requires more than a little patience. Instead, fold the ends over like an egg roll and make a roll; fasten each roll together with a couple of toothpicks through the flap.

Notes: Packaged turkey cutlets are readily available in the poultry section of the supermarket, or you can buy a whole breast and slice your own.

Unless you buy your sausages from an Italian specialty shop, they will probably be too big to roll up in a turkey cutlet, no matter how thin you pound it. If so, simply remove the sausage from its casing, or buy it in bulk if that's an option.

To keep fat content to a minimum, use the Italian-style turkey or chicken sausage now on the market, or combine equal measures of poultry sausage and plain ground pork.

Variation: Stuff the turkey cutlets with a moist mushroom filling. Soak 2 to 3 dried porcini mushrooms (*cèpes*) in hot water to cover for 30 minutes. Meanwhile, mince and sauté 1 pound fresh mushrooms in 4 tablespoons butter with 1 chopped shallot or 3 chopped scallions. Mix together with ¼ cup fresh bread crumbs moistened with chicken broth and/or the mushroom-soaking liquid (leaving the sediment in the bottom of the dish). Drain and chop the dried mushrooms. Season the mixture with salt and pepper to taste and stir in the dried mushrooms. Proceed with the recipe, omitting the olives. (This mushroom filling would also be good stuffed in large fresh mushroom caps with a little Parmesan on top and broiled. Or use it as a stuffing for a small Cornish hen.)

EDITORS' KITCHEN

These frankly rich "Swiss" enchiladas are always on the menu in Mexican restaurants, but we know hardly anyone who makes them at home. They're very easy and a wonderful way to use up leftover cooked turkey. Serve them with a side dish of black beans with onion or rice pilaf (page 189) with tomato and garlic.

Enchiladas Suizas

SERVES 6

Preheat the oven to 350°. Mince 1 cup of shredded cooked turkey in the food processor. In a bowl, mix together 2 more cups of shredded cooked turkey, 1 cup canned chopped green chilies, 3 pickled jalapeño peppers (seeded, rinsed, and minced), and 1 cup canned green chili sauce. Pour 1½ cups heavy cream into a shallow bowl. Have 12 corn tortillas ready to fry.

Heat 1 inch of oil in a small skillet. When the oil is just medium hot, slide one tortilla at a time into the oil and turn it over with tongs. Leave it in just long enough to soften. Remove it, letting the excess oil drip back into the skillet, and dip it into the cream, then place it in a baking dish.

Spoon some filling off center on the tortilla. Roll it up, rolling away from you, and turn it, flap side down, into place. Repeat with all the tortillas and filling. Drizzle with the remaining cream, cover with 1½ cups grated Monterey Jack, and sprinkle with 6 tablespoons pumpkin seeds. Bake for 15 to 20 minutes, or until the cheese melts. Sprinkle with chopped cilantro, if desired, and serve piping hot.

Grilled Beef Tenderloin with Roquefort and Red Pepper Butter

Camille Glenn

3 pounds beef tenderloin
Roquefort and Red Pepper Butter
    (recipe follows)
5 tablespoons butter
Salt and freshly ground black pepper
    to taste
2 tablespoons chopped fresh tarragon
    or 1 teaspoon dried tarragon
2 tablespoons chopped fresh parsley
Watercress or fresh spinach, for
    garnish

This tasty, beautiful, and simple recipe features some of America's favorite flavors—great beef, Roquefort cheese, and red peppers. It's a mouth-watering combination.

SERVES 6

*H*ave every particle of fat trimmed from the tenderloin. Let it stand, lightly covered, at room temperature for several hours before cooking.

Meanwhile, prepare the Roquefort and Red Pepper Butter.

When you are ready to cook, melt 4 tablespoons of the butter. Brush the meat well with butter and season with salt.

Barbecue the meat on a spit or on the grill (place an oiled rack 4 to 6 inches above medium-hot coals). In either case, it will take about 30 minutes for the tenderloin to cook to rare. (If cooking on a grill, turn it every 10 minutes.) It should register 125° on a meat thermometer for rare.

When the meat is done, remove it to a carving board and let it stand for 8 minutes. Sprinkle generously with salt, pepper, and fresh tarragon and parsley.

Carve the tenderloin into medium-thick slices and serve on warm plates garnished with watercress or fresh crisp spinach and several slices of Roquefort and Red Pepper Butter. Quickly spoon the juice that was released from carving the steak into a small pan. Heat it quickly with the remaining butter and add a touch of salt. Pour it over the steaks or serve in a sauceboat.

MAKES 1 CUP

Roquefort and Red Pepper Butter

1 small red bell pepper or 1 red sweet
    banana pepper
5 ounces Roquefort
1 cup (2 sticks) unsalted butter, at
    room temperature
Salt to taste
Cayenne pepper or Tabasco to taste
Hungarian paprika

*W*ash, core, and seed the red pepper. Cut it into wire-thin slivers.

Cream the Roquefort and butter together in a processor or with an electric mixer. Add the red pepper and blend. Season with salt and cayenne or Tabasco to taste.

Form the mixture into 2 balls and rotate them in paprika sprinkled on a piece of foil. Refrigerate to chill.

Serving Suggestions: Serve with garlic sautéed potatoes (page 170) and Stir-fried Green Beans (page 155).

Tips:

From Paula Wolfert: Rub oil and salt into your steak as soon as you bring it home from the market; the salt tenderizes the surface of the meat and helps give it a nice crust while the oil creates an air seal to protect the flavor.

Because tenderloin has so little fat, it dries out easily. The solution is to cut tenderloin steaks thick so that you can cook them rare.

Cut a pocket in a thick steak and tuck in a dab of soft Cheddar with crisp bacon and minced sun-dried tomatoes or a paste of mashed anchovy, garlic, and parsley.

Make plenty of the Roquefort and Red Pepper Butter and freeze what you don't need; use slices on pasta or atop a baked potato or a veal chop.

Note: Beef tenderloin seems like a very luxurious cut of beef, but it's really more economical than you might think, especially if you buy the whole tenderloin, trim it, and cut off your own steaks. Freeze what you don't use the first night, packaging the tail separately for a stir-fry meal and cutting the rest into family-size chunks—even a two-steak piece holds up better in the freezer than a single steak.

Variations:
Cut the meat into 1½-inch chunks, skewer them, and grill or sauté in butter. Serve as you would steaks.

Roast the whole tenderloin at 500° for 7 minutes per pound instead of grilling it.

Rub the tenderloin with olive oil, rosemary, thyme, salt, and cracked black pepper. Grill or roast. Garnish the outside of the roast with gremolata (minced parsley and garlic mixed with finely grated lemon zest).

From Patrick O'Connell at the Inn at Little Washington in Virginia: Serve "angels on horseback" (broiled oysters wrapped in bacon) to accompany a rare grilled tenderloin.

From Joyce Goldstein: Serve room temperature strips of grilled tenderloin over an arugula salad dressed with extra virgin olive oil, a touch of mellow red wine vinegar, salt, and cracked black pepper. (Goldstein's beef is home-cured with spices for 2 weeks.) Add thin slices of ricotta salata, an Italian table cheese available in specialty stores.

This is a fresh way to present familiar flavors. Peppers and onions in oil and vinegar are tried and true, and they make a great nest for the flank steak. Don't worry about the vinegar—this dish is not at all sour.

Grilled Flank Steak on a Bed of Roasted Peppers and Onions

Joyce Goldstein

SERVES 6 TO 8

*P*ut the steaks in a shallow nonaluminum container and sprinkle with 2 tablespoons olive oil, 1 tablespoon vinegar, and 2 teaspoons pepper. Cover and let marinate 2 hours at room temperature.

Preheat the oven to 400°. Rub the onions with 2 tablespoons oil and roast just until tender, about 1 hour. Halve and peel, then cut into 1-inch-wide slices.

Char the peppers over an open flame or under the broiler until blackened on all sides. Transfer to a plastic container with a lid or a paper or plastic bag. Cover the container or close the bag and let the peppers steam about 15 minutes. Peel the skins from the peppers; then cut the peppers in half, remove the stems, and scrape out the seeds. Cut into 1-inch-wide strips and toss with 2 tablespoons oil.

Heat the grill or broiler. Lightly sprinkle the steaks with salt and pepper and grill or broil 2 to 3 minutes each side for medium-rare.

Meanwhile, heat the sliced onions and peppers and remaining 2 tablespoons each oil and vinegar in a large

2 flank steaks, about 3 pounds total, trimmed well
8 tablespoons olive oil
3 tablespoons balsamic vinegar
2 teaspoons freshly ground pepper, plus additional to taste
6 large red onions
6 medium red peppers or combination red and yellow peppers
Salt

sauté pan or skillet over medium heat until warmed through, about 4 minutes. Season to taste with salt and pepper.

Slice the steaks across the grain on a slight diagonal. Make a bed of pepper and onions on each serving plate and top with the steak. Serve with fried potatoes.

Serving Suggestions: Serve with Potato Gratin (page 172) or Hot Devil Potatoes (page 175) and sautéed zucchini.

Tips:
Char the peppers directly over a charcoal fire while you're waiting for the coals to get hot enough to grill your steak. Let the peppers sit in a paper or plastic bag at least 5 minutes to loosen the skins before peeling.

Open a can of the excellent roasted peppers now on the market (Mancini is a good brand) if you have no time to grill your own; proceed with the recipe.

Cook the peppers and onions when you're grilling something earlier in the week; they will keep for at least a week in the refrigerator.

Note: Flank steak can be tough and stringy. Search out prime steaks for best results.

Spicy Skirt Steak with Cinnamon

Michael Roberts

Fajitas have made skirt steak more popular lately, which fits right in with our search for more flavor and more shopping value—though the more popular skirt steak becomes, the higher the price, we've noticed. It has a very "beefy" taste and, when quickly cooked and thinly sliced against the grain, it's quite tender. It's particularly good charcoal-grilled or broiled rare. This recipe makes enough sauce to reheat leftovers.

SERVES 2 TO 3

1 1¼- to 1½-pound skirt steak or flank steak

½ teaspoon salt

2 tablespoons roughly chopped onion

2 ripe plum tomatoes, roughly chopped (about ¼ pound)

1 cup veal stock or canned low-sodium beef broth

2 dried pasilla or ancho chili peppers or 2 teaspoons dried pasilla powder

2 jalapeño peppers or 1 serrano chili pepper, seeds removed

½ teaspoon ground cinnamon

2 tablespoons chopped cilantro

Pat the steak dry. Heat a heavy 12-inch skillet over high heat without oil and, when hot, add the meat. Sear well, about 2 minutes on each side.

Preheat oven to 200°.

Add the salt, onion, tomatoes, stock, dried peppers, jalapeño peppers, and cinnamon. Cook 5 minutes for medium-rare steak, turning once. For more well done steaks, reduce heat and cook longer. Remove steak to a platter and keep warm in oven while finishing the sauce.

Transfer contents of the skillet to a food processor or blender and puree until smooth. Strain through a sieve with large holes to remove seeds and skins. If the puree is too thin to make a sauce, return to skillet and cook over high heat, stirring, until it is reduced enough to coat the back of a spoon.

Remove steak from the oven and place on a cutting board. Thinly slice the steak, arrange on a warm serving platter, pour the sauce over, and sprinkle with chopped cilantro.

Serving Suggestions: Serve with Ten-minute Black Beans with Tomatoes and Coriander (page 187) and avocado and orange salad, and put out a bowl of tortilla chips.

Beef Braised in Coffee

(Stracotto al Caffè)

Jo Bettoja and Anna Maria Cornetto

1 teaspoon coarse salt

½ teaspoon freshly ground black
     pepper

4 pounds boneless lean beef rump
     roast

8 tablespoons (1 stick) unsalted butter

3 tablespoons corn oil

2½ cups thinly sliced red onion

¾ cup dry red wine

½ teaspoon sugar

¾ cup strongly brewed Italian
     espresso coffee

This rich-tasting beef dish has a mysterious complexity that comes from the wine and coffee braising liquid. Use a quality wine and espresso—it makes a big difference in this dish. This is an old family recipe from northern Italy, where they might be surprised to learn that the leftovers make excellent American barbecue sandwiches.

SERVES 6 TO 8

*P*ut the salt and pepper together in a saucer. Tie the meat so it will keep its shape and rub it with the salt and pepper.

Melt the butter with the corn oil in a flameproof 12-inch casserole with a lid. Add the onion and cook, uncovered, on low heat for 30 minutes, stirring frequently.

Turn up the heat slightly and brown the meat on all sides for 20 to 30 minutes, turning occasionally. Add the wine and let it evaporate for 5 minutes. Dissolve the sugar in the coffee and add to the meat.

Seal the casserole tightly with aluminum foil and place the lid on top. Simmer for 5 hours, basting and turning the meat once every hour.

Remove the meat from the casserole and let stand at room temperature for 10 minutes. Remove the string and slice thin, using an electric knife if possible. Arrange slices on a warm platter. Strain the sauce and pour over the meat. Serve hot.

Serving Suggestions: Serve with sautéed polenta (page 195) or herbed mashed potatoes (page 166).

Tip: Buy a premium-quality rump roast, the more marbling the better.

Variations:

Use half onions and half sliced fennel.

Increase the onions by 1 cup and use 1 cup *each* wine and espresso, adding 1 teaspoon sugar to the coffee, to increase the amount of sauce. You'll still wish you had more.

Don't bother straining the sauce.

Shred any leftover meat and mix it with a little of the onion sauce to moisten. Add a touch of liquid mesquite smoke and enough of your favorite barbecue sauce to make a flavorful sandwich filling. Serve on toasted buns.

Add 6 garlic cloves, 1 tablespoon ground cumin, 1 tablespoon chili powder, and 3 dried ancho chilies, stemmed and seeded, and substitute beef broth for the red wine. Use lard for browning the meat and precooking the onions. Puree the sauce after the meat is cooked. Serve with Mexican beans and rice. Use any leftovers for burritos or tacos.

Wild Mushroom Meat Loaf

Miriam Ungerer

1½ pounds lean ground beef
1 pound ground pork shoulder (fatty)
1 pound lean ground veal
⅓ cup bourbon
2 teaspoons coarse black pepper
2 ounces dried black Japanese mushrooms (Matsutakes)
1 ounce dried French chanterelles
1 cup minced onions
2 garlic cloves, minced
2 tablespoons butter
½ cup soft fresh white bread crumbs
1 large egg, beaten
¼ cup minced fresh parsley
½ teaspoon dried thyme
3 teaspoons salt
4 to 5 thin strips Virginia bacon (best quality, cut from slab)
Watercress

There's a long tradition of elegant meat loaves, but this one seems to us particularly tempting. The dried mushrooms are costly; on the other hand, you're not adding that much per person to the cost of an otherwise economical dish. We feel the splurge is well worth it.

SERVES 6

*M*ix together the beef, pork, veal, bourbon, and black pepper, cover with plastic wrap, and refrigerate overnight or several hours at least.

Wash the mushrooms well because they are apt to be a bit sandy. Put them in a deep narrow bowl and pour boiling water over them. Let stand 20 minutes. Save the water to use in soup. Drain the mushrooms, dry them, and cut out the hard centers of the Japanese type and just the very tips of the chanterelles. Chop these into about ¼-inch dice and add them to the meats.

Preheat oven to 350°.

Sauté the onions and garlic in the butter until limp and add them to the meats along with all remaining ingredients except the bacon and watercress. Mix the meat loaf well, using your hands and a light, quick motion. Do not squeeze the meat because this will make the meat loaf tough, and do not use a dough hook because this beats all life out of it. Shape the loaf into a long oval about 4 inches high. Put into a low-sided gratin dish and cover the meat loaf firmly with as many bacon strips as required. Place this in the center of the preheated oven and bake for 1 hour, or until an instant-read thermometer registers 170°. Do not overbake, or all the flavor and juiciness will stay behind in the pan juices. Let the meat loaf rest at least half an hour before serving. It is fine served at room temperature, but this is not highly spiced enough to be served cold. Slice in ½-inch servings, put the loaf back together tightly, and serve it on a platter surrounded by sprigs of watercress, lots of it.

Serving Suggestions: Serve with Skillet Scallions (page 178) and Baked Potatoes (page 164) or Pureed Parsnips (page 161).

Tip: Sauté vegetables before adding them to a meat loaf; the moisture of raw vegetables may exude and cause it to break and crumble.

Variation: Substitute fresh cultivated mushrooms for some of the dried. Replace ½ ounce of the chanterelles with 1 cup finely minced cremini mushrooms. Sauté the mushrooms and squeeze them dry in a paper towel, then add them to the meats.

Veal Scallops with Fennel
(Escalopes de veau au fenouil)

Elizabeth David

A truly unusual way to prepare veal scallops, which seem to have been left behind in the American food revolution. It's true that they're expensive, but they're also delicious and lean. This light, elegant, extremely easy dish depends on finding very good veal. The delicate taste and aroma of the fennel leaves is a perfect finish.

Brown scallops of veal in pork drippings or butter. Add 2 or 3 scallions for each scallop; cover the pan and simmer for 7 to 8 minutes. Throw in a handful of finely chopped fennel leaves, stir, and add a squeeze of lemon. Excellent.

Serving Suggestions: Serve with Pilaf (page 189) and Wondrous Carrots (page 141). Potato Gratin (page 172) would be a good choice for a low-calorie meal.

Tips:

Don't have the scallops pounded paper thin, as for scaloppine, which cooks in just a couple of minutes. The scallops should be about ¼ inch thick.

Slice the fennel bulb and sauté it or use it for salads. You can also braise it with potatoes in butter and cream. For lighter fare, braise it in a little stock in the microwave; great with pork chops.

This recipe is not suited to veal chops, which are so expensive that they're best reserved for the grill, where they really shine. Marinate the chops in a simple olive oil and lemon vinaigrette with minced rosemary or thyme. Grill them just until they're pale pink inside. If you raise and lower the grill lid a few times during cooking, the chops will pick up a light smoky flavor.

Note: Since fennel leaves are rarely used in recipes, be certain to find a lightly trimmed bulb at your produce market.

The shanks are the most succulent of all veal cuts. Like all braised meats, veal shanks—sometimes called osso buco—*are hassle-free and, like all veal, versatile enough to go from the family table to the company buffet. They're also practical; leftovers make fine ragout sauces for pasta or fillings for stuffed vegetables—so make more than you need, which is one per person. And unlike other cuts of veal, the shank is reasonably priced. Best of all is the hind shank, which has even more of the rich and nutritious marrow.*

Veal Shanks

SERVES 4

Cut the white membrane around the outside edge of the shank, or the meat will curl up when it's cooked. If the shanks are very heavy and meaty, tie a string around the outside edge to keep the meat from falling completely away from the bone; remove the string before serving.

Brown 4 veal shanks in 3 tablespoons hot oil in a heavy skillet with a cover. After the shanks are nice and brown on both sides, lower the heat and sauté 2 minced garlic cloves and 1 minced onion in the pan drippings. Pour in ¼ cup white wine or dry vermouth and scrape up the browning bits. Add enough additional braising liquid (beef broth is ideal) to partly cover the meat a third of the way up. Cover and cook over low heat until the shanks are falling away from the bone. Add liquid if necessary; there should always be enough to cover the shanks about a third of the way up the sides. The braising time is 1 to 1½ hours, depending on the size and thickness of the shanks. Remove the meat, then reduce the pan juices over high heat until they're almost a glaze.

Season with salt and pepper and pour over the shanks. Serve immediately.

Tips:
From Lorenza de Medici: Add the braising liquid a little at a time so that the meat doesn't taste boiled.

Serve veal shanks as soon as possible after preparation; they do not store or reheat well.

Variations:
Use the white part of leeks, carefully cleaned and sliced, instead of the onion. Soak golden raisins in brandy while the meat is cooking. Add fresh or dried thyme to the braising liquid. After you have boiled down the braising liquid to a thick glaze, add some heavy cream and reduce that as well, stirring up all the pan juices into the cream sauce. Toss in the brandy-soaked raisins and splash the sauce with balsamic vinegar or lemon juice, just enough to take the rich edge from the cream. Be sure to salt and pepper adequately.

Use part beef broth and part marsala wine for the braising liquid. Add 2 drained and stemmed canned Italian plum tomatoes for every shank. Soak 1 ounce of dried porcini mushrooms (*cèpes*) in hot water for 30 minutes to soften them. Mince the mushrooms and add to the braising liquid along with the mushroom water, strained through a paper towel to remove any grit. To garnish the shanks, quickly sauté a few quartered fresh mushrooms in a hot skillet until they are just golden; dust them with minced parsley.

Roast Pork with Bay Leaves

(Arrosto di maiale all'alloro)

Marcella Hazan

Braising is usually reserved for tougher cuts of meat because slow cooking tenderizes them and helps to develop flavor. Pork is an exception; today's pork loin is tender enough, but it's so lean that the meat tends to seize up and taste dry when it's roasted at high temperatures.

We like this stove-top braising method very much: It's easy, it doesn't heat up the entire kitchen, and it's particularly well suited to pork.

SERVES 6

2 pounds boneless pork loin
3 tablespoons butter
2 tablespoons vegetable oil
Salt
1 teaspoon whole peppercorns
3 medium bay leaves
½ cup red-wine vinegar

Choose a good heavy pot, preferably enameled cast iron, just large enough to contain the meat, and provided with a close-fitting lid. Heat the butter and oil together at medium-high heat. When the butter foam begins to subside, put in the meat and brown it well on all sides.

When the meat is well browned, salt it on all sides, then add the peppercorns, bay leaves, and vinegar. Turn up the heat for as long as it takes to scrape up all the cooking residue from the bottom. (Do not allow the vinegar to evaporate more than slightly.) Turn the heat down to low, cover the pot, and cook slowly for at least 2 hours, until a fork easily pierces the meat. (Check from time to time to make sure that the liquid in the pot has not completely dried up. If it has, you can add, as required, 2 or 3 tablespoons of water.)

Place the meat on a cutting board and cut into slices ¼ to ⅜ inch thick. Arrange the slices, slightly overlapping, on a warm serving platter.

Tip the pot, removing most, but not all, of the fat with a spoon. Remove the bay leaves and pour the sauce from the pot over the meat. (If there should be any cooking residue in the bottom of the pot, put in 2 tablespoons of water and scrape it loose over high heat. Add to the sauce.)

Serving Suggestions: Serve with Big Baked Onions (page 158) and Wondrous Carrots (page 141), or start with one of the skillet pastas (pages 27–28) and accompany the roast with Cauliflower with Raisins and Pine Nuts (page 142).

Variation: Use balsamic vinegar instead of red wine vinegar; it's unusual and produces a mysterious taste.

This Tuscan dish is incredibly easy to make and tastes as wonderful at room temperature as it does right out of the oven. In fact, it only improves with age.

Succulent Pork Roast with Fennel
(Arista)

Viana La Place and Evan Kleiman

SERVES 6 TO 8

6 garlic cloves, peeled and minced
1 to 2 tablespoons fennel seeds
2 teaspoons coarse salt
Freshly ground pepper to taste
1 boneless pork rib roast (about
   4 pounds)
Fruity olive oil

*M*ake a paste with the minced garlic, fennel, salt, and pepper in a mortar and pestle, or mash with the side of a chef's knife. If the roast is rolled and tied, unroll it. Spread most of the paste over the meat, reserving a tablespoon or so. Roll and tie the roast so that the white tenderloin is more or less in the center, surrounded by the darker meat of the loin. Make a few incisions with a sharp knife about ½ inch deep in the roast and stuff some of the paste into them. Rub any remaining paste over the outside of the meat. Rub a little olive oil over the meat and place in a roasting pan. Roast, uncovered, in a preheated 350° oven about 2 hours, or until the internal temperature registers 170° on a meat thermometer. Baste the roast two or three times with the pan juices. Remove the roast from the oven and allow to cool. When it is tepid, cut into ½-inch-thick slices and drizzle a little fruity olive oil over the meat if desired.

Serving Suggestions: This country-style roast tastes best with equally earthy accompaniments, such as Big Baked Onions (page 158), Slow-baked Tomatoes (page 181), fried polenta (page 195), or mashed potatoes with garlic and herbs (page 166).

Tips:
Crush the fennel seeds in a minichopper if you have one, then add the garlic, salt, and pepper.

Take the prepared paste to the butcher and ask him to select, season, and tie the roast for you. Be sure to save a little of the paste for rubbing the outside of the roast when you get home.

From Julia Child: Butterfly the pork roast instead of rolling it; it cuts the cooking time in half. Spread the roast out and slash through the thickest parts to even out the cooking surface. Make cross-hatch slashes in the fat and rub it with coarse salt. Push the seasoning paste into ½-inch slits in the surface of the meat and smear the rest in the crevices. Roast the pork, fat side down, in a pre-heated 375° oven for 1 hour, or until the internal temperature reaches 140°. Baste with pan drippings every 20 minutes and turn the roast fat side up on the final basting. Finish the roast under the broiler.

Do this preliminary roasting somewhat ahead, but don't leave it longer than a couple of hours. Broil the meat 3 inches from the heat for about 10 minutes on each side, which should bring the temperature to the perfect 160°. Let the roast rest for 10 minutes before carving on the diagonal.

Note: Be sure to ask for the *center-cut rib loin* for this recipe. A regular loin roast, which the butcher will probably suggest instead, will be too dry. The important thing is for the white meat to be in the center of the roast with the dark meat rolled around it.

Variations:

Substitute a paste of Roasted Garlic (page 151) and minced fresh (or crumbled dried) rosemary for the garlic and fennel paste.

Marinate a rolled pork roast overnight in white wine seasoned with a sliced onion, a bay leaf, thyme sprigs, and several whole cloves, as they do in the Provençal Alps. If you don't want to use fennel seeds, tuck fresh sage leaves into small slits cut into the surface of the meat.

Serve leftover pork, thinly sliced, with a thin-noodle salad with spicy peanut sauce. Also good as accompaniments are chick peas mixed with yogurt and mint or a dollop of hot mango chutney with a rice pilaf prepared with currants, onion, and slivered almonds (page 189).

Sliver the leftover meat and mix it with canned Mexican green chilies, a little bottled hot salsa, and grated Monterey Jack; roll the mixture up in a warm flour tortilla for a great burrito. Serve with refried black beans with sour cream, chopped scallions, and some fresh cilantro on the side.

Pork Slices with Prunes

(Noisette de porc aux pruneaux)

Curnonsky

This classic French dish from the Loire is proof that pork can be as elegant as veal. The unctuous prune and cream sauce makes this fit for a special occasion. Even those who don't like prunes will love it. With the microwave as sous-chef, you can now put this recipe together in no time.

SERVES 8

3 cups dried prunes (about 1¼ pound)

1¼ cups Vouvray or other semidry wine

Flour

2½-pound pork tenderloin or boneless pork loin, trimmed of all fat and cut into 8 slices

4 tablespoons butter

Salt and pepper

1 tablespoon currant jelly

2 cups heavy cream

Soak the prunes overnight in the wine.

The next day, bring the prunes and wine to a simmer and cook them gently for 30 minutes. Alternatively, poach the prunes in the wine in a 300° oven in a covered baking dish for 1 hour, or until they are plump and tender.

Coat the pork slices lightly with flour, heat the butter in a skillet, and sauté the pork until it is golden brown on both sides. Season the slices with salt and pepper as they cook. When the pork is tender, in about 5 or 6 minutes, transfer it to a warmed serving dish.

Arrange the prunes around the pork and pour the prune cooking liquid into the skillet. Stir to deglaze, and reduce the liquid until it is syrupy. Stir in the currant jelly, then add the cream, bring to a boil, and reduce this sauce, if necessary, until it thickens slightly. Correct the seasoning, pour the sauce over the pork, and serve hot.

Serving Suggestions: Serve with Sautéed-Braised Chanterelles (page 157) or braised small white onions and Nutty Rice (page 190).

Tips:

From Madeleine Kamman: Freeze pork for 12 days before cooking it to be safe when cooking it pink.

Use pork tenderloin rather than loin slices; it will be sweeter and more tender, and it will cook a little faster.

Use the microwave to cook the prunes and wine. Cover them and cook on high, in 6-minute intervals, until they're plump and tender as the recipe directs. If you forgot to soak the prunes overnight, just zap them a bit longer.

Variations:

Omit the prunes and follow the recipe down to the deglazing procedure, using chicken broth as the liquid. Sliding the pan off the fire for a minute, whisk in equal parts herb or peppercorn mustard to taste (about 1 table-spoon per serving). Add a pat of butter if you aren't getting a smooth blend. Go back to the fire—heat the pan and whisk again. Add the heavy cream and some snipped chives or minced scallions and briskly reduce the mustard cream until it's just thick enough to coat the pork. If you like, add 1 or 2 tablespoons freshly grated Parmesan (or aged Monterey Jack) to the cream before it's completely thickened.

Try Turkish dried apricots instead of prunes. Soak them in the wine and substitute apricot preserves for the currant jelly. Add a pinch of pulverized saffron to the cream reduction, and you have moved this dish considerably southeast of the Loire Valley.

For dedicated improvisational cooks: Add a pinch of ground ginger and cinnamon to the cream reduction, along with the saffron, and you will have taken pork about as far as it can go toward the Moslem world.

Pork Tenderloin

This tasty, lean little roast is very quick cooking and handy to store in the freezer for impromptu dinners. It's also excellent grilled, using your favorite marinade. We especially like a ginger-soy-honey-garlic combination mixed with Chinese or Thai chili sauce. And Williams-Sonoma's Special Selection BBQ Sauce is perfect for pork tenderloin.

SERVES 2 TO 4

Tuck the thinner tail end of the tenderloin under to form a roast of even thickness. Tie it up with kitchen string at three or four intervals across the width of the meat or fasten the tail with toothpicks. Marinate the meat as long as overnight or as briefly as 1 hour, reserving some sauce for basting during cooking. To self-baste the roast, wrap 2 or 3 strips of smoked bacon around it and fasten them with toothpicks before marinating or coating with sauce.

Preheat the oven to 375°.

Roast the meat for 45 minutes, basting frequently to keep it from drying out. When the tenderloin is cooked (160°), pour off the excess fat and keep the pork warm until you're ready to serve it. Deglaze the roasting pan on top of the stove, using a jigger of brandy, calvados, or bourbon and some chicken stock to scrape up the drippings. Scrape and stir over high heat until a little glazing liquid forms to pour over the sliced meat.

PORK CHOPS

If dry-roasting a pork loin can often be disappointing, your chances of producing a tough, dry loin chop are even greater.

We find the best method of braising pork chops is James Beard's, described below. Stuffing pork chops also helps to keep them moist.

We prefer to use bacon fat or lard for sautéing pork chops because it returns some of the flavor to the pork. If lard sounds alarming, take comfort from Paula Wolfert, who points out that according to the USDA lard has less than half the cholesterol of butter.

Brown the chops in a cast-iron skillet over medium heat for 5 minutes on each side, resisting the urge to turn the heat to high. Cover and braise in chicken broth or dry white wine or, in the case of chutney-stuffed chops (below), in a little tart fruit juice.

James Beard's Braised Pork Chops

Brown the chops in a skillet, then transfer them to a microwavesafe casserole with a lid. Deglaze the skillet with the braising liquid to get all the tasty bits and pour over the meat. Cover and cook on high for 10 minutes for 4 chops.

Microwave-braised Pork Chops

Select chops at least 1½ inches thick. Have the butcher cut a pocket or do it yourself by cutting horizontally halfway through the chop. Rub the inside of the pocket with black-olive paste (*olivada*), then push in a little creamy ricotta mixed with Roasted Garlic (page 151).

A good bottled chutney makes another tasty quick stuffing, as do prune butter and apricot or ginger preserves.

Stuffed Pork Chops

Sicilian Meatballs with Raisins and Pine Nuts

(Polpette alla siciliana)

Jo Bettoja and Anna Maria Cornetto

1½ pounds pork, ground twice
1 egg plus 1 egg yolk
Grated zest of 1 lemon
¼ cup dark or light raisins
4½ tablespoons pine nuts
1½ amaretti cookies, crushed and
    softened in 2½ tablespoons milk
⅛ teaspoon ground cinnamon
1½ teaspoons salt
½ teaspoon freshly ground black
    pepper
½ cup peanut oil
3 tablespoons sugar
½ cup white wine vinegar

Who says meatballs have to be plebeian? These moist, delectable pork morsels have that indigenous sweet-sour Sicilian tang and are ideal for casual entertaining. They can even be made the night before and successfully reheated.

SERVES 6

Combine the meat, egg, egg yolk, lemon zest, raisins, pine nuts, amaretti, cinnamon, salt, and pepper; mix well, with your hands, if desired.

Wetting your hands with cold water, form small meatballs about the size of Ping-Pong balls. Take care that all the pine nuts are tucked well into the meat and do not protrude.

Heat the oil in a large skillet and brown the meatballs all over, then with a slotted spoon remove them to another pan. Add the sugar and vinegar and cook until the vinegar evaporates, shaking the pan occasionally. Serve hot.

Serving Suggestions: Serve with a simple side dish of angel hair pasta tossed with olive oil, finely minced garlic, and salt and pepper or grilled polenta (page 195) and Baked Red Beets (page 136).

Tips:
Do not let the vinegar evaporate completely if you make the meatballs ahead of time; you'll want some liquid left when you reheat them. (We tripled the quantity of sauce specified in the recipe and had none too much.)

Shape meatballs (and hamburgers, for that matter) very gently, just enough to hold them together when they hit the heat. For keeping ground meat mixtures light and moist, be careful not to compact them.

Variations:

Use a slice of good crustless bread if you can't find amaretti cookies. Soak it in a little milk, then squeeze it dry.

Use the meatball mixture to stuff large mushrooms for a good first course to serve before a meatless main dish pasta or bean dish. Lightly oil mushroom caps, then press some meat into them, rounding off the tops. Broil on a sheet of foil, basting once or twice with the drippings. The mushrooms should be done in about 10 minutes. While they cook, make the vinegar and sugar syrup separately, following the recipe. Drizzle the hot mushrooms with the glaze just before serving.

Ham Baked in Cola

James Beard

Yankees sometimes think this recipe is just a bad joke, but you really have to try it—all the great southern cooks agree that it's wonderful. Besides, there's something as charming as bobbing for apples about the very idea of dunking a whole ham in Coke. It's hard to imagine a simpler recipe, and except for the ham, the ingredients are pantry staples.

*P*lace the ham, fat side down, in a roasting pan. Add cola to half-cover the ham. Bake at 350°, allowing 15 minutes per pound. Baste the ham frequently with the cola. Remove the ham from the pan, skin it, and rub well with dry mustard, pepper, bread crumbs, and brown sugar. Press the coating into the fat. Place the ham on a rack, return to a 350° oven for 35 to 40 minutes, and baste with cola.

1 tenderized ham, about 10 pounds
Cola
2 teaspoons dry mustard
1 teaspoon freshly ground pepper
1½ cups bread crumbs
1 cup brown sugar

Serving Suggestions: Serve with Early Summer Fresh Corn Pudding (page 146) or Cheese Grits (page 195) or Spoon Bread (page 197).

Tip: Taste your dry mustard for sharpness; you may need to increase the amount if it's been on the shelf for a long time.

Note: Be sure to choose a ham with at least a thin layer of fat between the skin and the meat. You will need that to properly coat the ham with the crumb crust.

Variation: Substitute hard cider for the cola or use equal parts dry white wine and sweet cider.

EDITORS' KITCHEN

Ham Steaks

What to do with those appealingly easy, ready-to-cook, packaged ham steaks? In our opinion, fry equals dry, so we simmer them in a flavoring liquid, such as dry white wine, vermouth, Madeira, red wine, or port. Apple cider or fresh orange juice will lend a lovely fruity essence. Broth or beer will also do.

SERVES 1 TO 2

Remove the rind or slash the ham steak at 1-inch intervals around the edge to keep it from curling up—or do as Julia Child does and cut it into serving pieces to begin with.

Heat a skillet and lightly sauté the steak in hot fat (butter, butter and oil, or just oil). When it's slightly brown, add enough flavoring liquid to come halfway up the thickness of the steak. Simmer gently, uncovered, for 5 to 10 minutes, depending on the thickness of the meat. The ham is precooked, so all you need to do is infuse it with flavor and keep it moist.

Remove the meat and keep it warm while you reduce the liquid in the pan over medium-high heat until you have a nice, syrupy glaze to spoon over the ham. If you use fruit juice, add a drizzle of honey to the pan juices before reducing it. A dash of cayenne will temper the sweetness.

Variation: Use port or Madeira and add a splash of heavy cream to the pan juices along with a squeeze of tomato paste from a tube. Sauté sliced mushrooms in butter with chopped scallions and add to the reduced sauce.

Church-Supper Ham Loaf

Marcia Adams

1 pound ground ham
1 pound lean sausage, at room
    temperature
2 cups soft bread crumbs
2 eggs
1 cup sour cream
⅓ cup chopped onion
2 tablespoons lemon juice
1 teaspoon curry powder
1 teaspoon ground ginger
1 teaspoon powdered mustard
⅛ tablespoon grated nutmeg
⅛ teaspoon paprika

BASTING SAUCE

1 cup brown sugar
½ cup water
½ cup cider vinegar
¼ teaspoon black pepper

Now we're really sorry we missed all those church suppers! This Amish country meat loaf is truly unusual, well seasoned and suitable for both family and company.

SERVES 8 TO 10

*P*reheat oven to 350°. In a large mixing bowl, lightly but thoroughly combine the meats and crumbs; use your hands if necessary. In a medium bowl, beat the eggs and add the sour cream, onion, lemon juice, and spices. Mix well, pour over the meat mixture, and blend. Form mixture into a loaf and place in an oiled 9 × 13-inch baking dish. Bake uncovered for 1 hour.

Meanwhile, prepare the basting sauce. In a small saucepan, combine the brown sugar with the remaining ingredients and bring to a boil. When the loaf has baked for 45 minutes, remove from oven and drain the excess fat. Pour the sauce over the loaf and continue baking for 15 minutes, basting now and then with the pan juices.

Serving Suggestions: Serve with Oven-fried Sweet Potatoes (page 169) and Braised Garlic and String Beans (page 153).

Tips:
Be sure to use the large baking dish; it allows the fat to drain and gives the basting sauce the room it needs to fully glaze the sides of the loaf as well as the top.

Double the curry, ginger, and mustard; it makes the loaf even better. The Amish might frown on such extravagance, but the surprising flavors make this dish sing.

Use leftover baked ham but not country ham; only a tenderized ham will work here.

Roast Lamb with Monsieur Henny's Potato, Onion, and Tomato Gratin

(Gigot rôti au gratin de Monsieur Henny)

Patricia Wells

There's an atavistic pleasure to this dish, in which the delectable juices from the roasting lamb drip slowly into the succulent vegetables lying in a bed beneath it. Best of all, it's a one-dish meal—all the company it needs is a sturdy red wine and some French bread.

SERVES 8 TO 10

6 garlic cloves, 1 clove split, the rest chopped
2 pounds baking potatoes, such as russets, peeled and very thinly sliced
Salt and freshly ground black pepper
1 tablespoon fresh thyme
2 large onions, very thinly sliced
5 medium tomatoes (about 1 pound), cored and thinly sliced
2/3 cup dry white wine
1/3 cup extra virgin olive oil
1 leg of lamb, bone-in (6 to 7 pounds)

Preheat the oven to 400°.

Rub the bottom of a large oval porcelain gratin dish, about 16 × 10 × 2 inches, with the split garlic clove. Arrange the potatoes in a single layer. Season generously with the salt, pepper, and some of the thyme and chopped garlic. Layer the sliced onions on top; season as with the potatoes. Layer the tomatoes on top of the onions. Season with salt, pepper, and the remaining thyme and garlic. Pour on the white wine and then the oil.

Trim the thicker portions of fat from the leg of lamb. Season the meat with salt and pepper. Place a sturdy cake rack or oven rack directly on top of the gratin dish. Set the lamb on the rack so that the juices will drip into the gratin.

Roast, uncovered, for about 1 hour and 15 minutes for rare lamb. (For well-done lamb, roast an additional 30 to 40 minutes.) Turn the lamb every 15 minutes, basting it with liquid from the dish underneath. Remove from the oven and let the lamb sit for 20 minutes before carving.

To serve, carve the lamb into thin slices and arrange on warmed dinner plates or on a serving platter, with the vegetable gratin alongside.

Tips:

Always have your meat at room temperature before cooking, or your timing may be way off. This is particularly important for roasts that need to be cooked rare to pink.

Remember to preheat the oven for 15 to 20 minutes to the selected temperature. Richard Sax says that sealing the juices into a roast by starting it off at a higher temperature is a myth. But it does produce a nice crusty exterior that we agree lends texture and character to the meat.

The easiest way to turn a roast over is with very fast hands, each protected with a wad of paper towels or foil. Avoid piercing the meat with a fork, or you'll lose the delectable natural juices.

Variations:

We find it difficult to think of roast lamb without rosemary. If you feel the same, poke some rosemary needles into the surface of this roast, if only to provide that heavenly aroma.

Try stuffing the lamb with a mixture of feta and chopped pistachios; another great combination is Chèvre mixed with chopped sun-dried tomatoes packed in oil.

Omit the tomatoes when they are not in season or sub–stitute roasted red pepper strips to get the color, taste, and look of Provence; imported roasted peppers in cans or jars are fine for this. Increase the white wine to 1 cup to compensate for the lack of tomato juices.

Soak rolled anchovy fillets in milk for 30 minutes to sweeten them, then scatter them sparingly in the layer of chopped garlic, or poke them into surface slashes in the meat. Take care when you add salt to the recipe.

From James Beard: an intriguing Swedish leg of lamb. Rub the meat with salt, pepper, and thyme, roast on a rack for 30 minutes, then baste periodically with a cup of European-strength breakfast coffee *with* cream and sugar. (A couple of tablespoons of brandy wouldn't hurt a bit.) When the meat is done, skim the fat, adjust the seasonings, and serve the coffee pan juices over the meat. Using coffee as a cooking liquid spans continents. It's especially delicious in roast turkey gravy and adds a new dimension to braised beef (see page 90).

Moghul Roasted Leg of Lamb

(Raan Saag)

Jennifer Brennan

This is a truly wonderful recipe, full of fragrant sweet spices and mellow flavors—an aristocratic dish from the court days in India. The long ingredients list may look intimidating, but in fact it takes more time to read it than it does to put the dish together. Just remember to start a couple of days ahead, or see the quick-fix tip at the end of the marinade recipe.

SERVES 8 TO 10

1 6-pound leg of lamb, the skin (fell) and fat removed, boned, and but-terflied (the butcher will normally do this for you and tie the meat together)

1 2-inch piece fresh gingerroot, peeled and minced

3 teaspoons salt

½ teaspoon ground cardamom

½ teaspoon ground cinnamon

¼ teaspoon ground cloves

½ teaspoon freshly ground black pepper

½ teaspoon freshly grated nutmeg

1 teaspoon cayenne pepper

2 tablespoons lemon juice

1 teaspoon cumin seeds

1 teaspoon vegetable oil

Yogurt Marinade (recipe follows)

Make numerous deep slits in the entire surface of the lamb flesh with the point of a knife.

Combine the ginger, all the remaining ground spices, the lemon juice, and the seeds in a blender. Blend on high speed to a smooth and even sauce. Add the vegetable oil at intervals to lubricate the mixture.

Pour the ingredients from the blender onto the lamb and press the mixture into the slits.

Prepare the Yogurt Marinade and marinate the lamb. Preheat the oven to 450°.

Roast the meat with its marinade in a covered casserole for about 30 minutes. Reduce the oven temperature to 350° and continue to cook for another 2 hours and 15 minutes, stirring occasionally, until the meat is just tender but cooked through.

Combine all the ingredients in a food processor with a blade and blend them on high for about 20 seconds.

Pour and massage the Yogurt Marinade onto the lamb. Place the entire mixture in a tightly sealed plastic bag and refrigerate for about 2 days. You may hasten the marinating process by leaving the bag at room temperature for about 3 hours.

Serving Suggestions: Serve with Spinach Pilaf (page 192) and Roasted Onions with Sage (page 159), omitting the sage. Garnish the onions with currants plumped in the balsamic vinegar specified in the recipe.

Tips:
Dry the meat very well with paper towels before rubbing it with the dry spices; they will form a little "crust" on the meat and help the wet marinade adhere.

Mix the dry spices with the oil in a mortar with a pestle, or if you have a minichopper, pulverize the dry spices and seeds in it, then add the lemon juice and oil to make a paste.

Variations: Cook the untied butterflied lamb on the grill instead of roasting it. To even out the cooking time between the thick and thin sections of the roast, slash neatly into the thick parts to allow the heat to penetrate. Lower and raise the lid on the grill a few times to achieve a subtle smoky taste. Cook until faintly pink at the center of the thickest part.

Yogurt Marinade

½ cup plain yogurt
¼ cup sour cream
¼ cup blanched almonds
2 tablespoons shelled pistachios
1 teaspoon saffron threads, soaked
    for 10 minutes in 2 tablespoons
    hot water
1½ tablespoons honey

Rack of Lamb with Anise and Sweet Garlic

Michele Urvater and David Liederman

2 racks of lamb, about 8 chops each
Coarse salt
Freshly ground pepper
2¼ teaspoons anise seed
2 heads garlic, cloves separated but
    unpeeled
½ tablespoon sugar
2 tablespoons red-wine vinegar

This is a particularly unusual treatment of rack of lamb. This cut of meat really needs nothing more than its traditional coating of fine bread crumbs mixed with rosemary, garlic, salt, pepper, and olive oil, but here is a refreshing alternative.

SERVES 4

Preheat the oven to 425°.

Season the meat with coarse salt, pepper, and 1 teaspoon of anise seed per rack of lamb. Place the racks of lamb without a roasting rack in one roasting pan if you have a large one, or 2 smaller ones. Strew garlic around the lamb and roast for 45 minutes for rarish lamb or 55 minutes for medium.

Remove the meat from the oven and place it on a carving board to rest.

With a slotted spoon, remove the garlic cloves from the roasting pan, and pop the flesh out of the skins into a 7-inch skillet. Add ¼ teaspoon anise seed to the same skillet, along with the sugar and vinegar.

Bring all of this to a boil and reduce rapidly until the sugar and liquid turn viscous and syrupy and coat the garlic. Season with salt and pepper.

Slice the racks into chops. Serve 3 to 4 lamb chops per person on warmed dinner plates. Spoon some garlic and sauce around the chops and serve.

Serving Suggestions: Serve with crispy shoestring potatoes (frozen ones are fine if fried in a shallow amount of oil) and Slow-baked Tomatoes (page 181) with capers.

Tips:

Cook the garlic cloves in their skins; it makes them very sweet and soft. Don't be put off by the amount specified; it really won't be too much.

Rack of lamb is usually sitting in the specialty meat case at the supermarket, fully prepared for roasting and serving. If you are not so fortunate, ask your butcher to trim the meat from the ends of the rib bones and be sure the chine bone is sawed through so that you can easily slice your roast into one-rib servings.

A rack of lamb is usually seven ribs; since the meat on each rib is minimal, one rack will feed only three people, sometimes only two, depending on size.

Roast a rack of lamb on your charcoal grill. By raising and lowering the lid on the grill, you can give the lamb a slightly smoky taste and also maintain its moisture perfectly.

Lamb and Olive Balls

Maggie Blyth Klein

What better proof of how good a succulent meatball can be—in any cuisine!

3 slices bread, country-style white or
    whole wheat
2 pounds fairly lean ground lamb
¼ pound feta, crumbled
1 cup kalamata olives, pitted and
    chopped
1 egg, beaten
½ tablespoon cinnamon
½ teaspoon hot red-pepper flakes
3 garlic cloves, crushed
1 bunch cilantro, chopped
3 tablespoons olive oil

MAKES 10 MEATBALLS; SERVES 8 TO 10

Cut the crusts from the bread; soak the slices in water, wring them out, and crumble them. With your fingers, mix the lamb well with the bread, feta, olives, egg, cinnamon, hot-pepper flakes, garlic, and cilantro. Form into 10 large meatballs.

In a heavy frying pan, cook the meatballs in the olive oil until crisp and brown on one side; then turn and brown the balls on all sides, no more than 10 minutes, over a fairly high heat. The meat should be rare.

Serving Suggestions: Serve with orzo and Slow-baked Tomatoes (page 181).

Tip: To pit kalamata olives, which are soft, just press down on them with your thumb and the pits will come right out, or use a pitter.

Note: Have the butcher trim and grind some lean lamb meat for you; the ground lamb found in supermarket packages is often too fatty.

Variations:
Omit the cilantro or substitute a mixture of minced scallions, parsley, and dill.

Make twice as many meatballs from this recipe, 20 meatballs about the size of a large lime.

Make the meatballs cocktail size and serve them with Herbed Yogurt Cheese Dip (page 8).

• PASTA •

EDITORS' KITCHEN

It's hard to think of a more satisfying way to assuage hunger than sitting down to a warm bowl of well-prepared pasta. In the twelve minutes or so it takes to cook the pasta, you can toss together a salad, chunk-cut a crusty loaf of peasant bread, set the table, pour the wine, and assemble a plate of fresh fruit and a basket of cookies or biscotti—a great meal in just minutes. (Don't forget the espresso!)

Pasta as a company main dish is best reserved for casual entertaining, but there are occasions when a pasta supper is just right. If you want to extend the meal for guests, start off one of the seafood pasta dishes with an antipasto or a platter of mixed sautéed sweet peppers or selection of steamed vegetables served at room temperature with a vinaigrette. Cheese or vegetable pasta is wonderful preceded by a skillet of garlicky scampi spiked with hot-pepper flakes (pages 50–51) or a steamy bowl of mussels flecked with herbs. Crispy strips of pan-fried fish (page 62) with lots of lemon wedges or paper-thin slices of prosciutto and fresh smoked mozzarella are all good ways to herald a hot bowl of perfect pasta.

Of the hundreds of pasta recipes we culled, we found the ones we've selected particularly interesting. Any one of them in small portions would also make an excellent company starter.

HOW TO COOK PASTA

The key to cooking pasta successfully is selecting the right pasta to begin with—a good-quality imported dried one (DeCecco and Martini are excellent) or fresh pasta from a reliable source. Pasta standards are strict in Italy, where hard durum wheat is the rule. Select one that's the right shape for the sauce. Rule of thumb: The thicker the sauce, the larger the pasta.

Pasta should be cooked until it's firm enough to support the sauce it's carrying, so that it still has a little resistance to the bite—the stage called al dente. Overcooked pasta absorbs too much of the sauce and becomes mushy. Remember that fresh pasta cooks in a fraction of the time it takes for dried pasta. Angel hair, the skinniest one, will be done in about a minute.

Here are some tips from the experts to help you make perfect pasta:

- From Fred Plotkin: Use a minimum of four quarts of water to a pound of pasta; the pot should never be more than three-quarters full.

- From Giuliano Bugialli: Start with cold water, since hot tap water has an off taste. When the water is boiling, add two tablespoons of salt per pound of pasta. This may seem like a lot, and in fact some other experts recommend just a pinch, but Bugialli says it takes that much to adequately flavor a pound of pasta. Put the lid back on the pot once you've added the pasta to bring it back to a boil as quickly as possible.

- From Christopher Styler: Keep the pot on a very gentle boil for filled pastas, like ravioli; the delicate pasta may split open during a furious boil. Use a little of the pasta cooking water if you need to thin out the sauce.

- From Viana La Place and Evan Kleiman: Cook the pasta at a steady boil, stirring every so often. Begin taste-testing it well before you think it's ready. Drain the pasta the minute it's done and sauce it right away, before it has a chance to stick together.

- From Elizabeth David: Use the method described on the Agnesi pasta boxes. Ms. David prefers this method to the ordinary one. Bring seven quarts of water to a boil, add three tablespoons of salt and a pound of pasta. After the water comes back to the boil, let it boil for three minutes, then turn off the heat. Cover the pan with a towel and its lid. Leave it for five to eight minutes, depending on the thickness of the pasta; for example, five minutes for spaghettini, eight minutes for short, fat tubes. The pasta should be just *al dente*. It works perfectly.

- From Jo Bettoja: Add the cheese to the drained pasta before it's sauced, as they do in Rome, where Ms. Bettoja lives; it makes a creamier, more flavorful dish. They also add a pinch of sugar to the tomato sauce to balance out the acid.

- From Arrigo Cipriani: Add the pasta to the pot in handfuls so that the water doesn't go completely off the boil. People think the pasta won't all be done at the same time if you add it by handfuls, but it all works out just fine.

- To all this expertise we would add one further note of advice: Serve the pasta immediately in warm shallow bowls. More than any other food we can think of, pasta suffers in cold serving plates.

Pasta with Gorgonzola

Deborah Madison

There are as many variations of this dish as there are Italian cookbooks, but this one has a particular charm: The sauce "cooks" directly in the pasta bowl as it's being warmed over the boiling pasta. Linguine or a short tubular pasta like penne work best in this dish.

Dolce latte Gorgonzola is perfect for this recipe. Otherwise, if your Gorgonzola is a bit on the strong side, smooth out the flavor with a little heavy cream, half-and-half, or mascarpone, as Alice Waters does.

½ pound dried pasta
1 garlic clove, thinly sliced
6 ounces Gorgonzola, more or less
2 tablespoons unsalted butter
Salt
Freshly ground pepper

SERVES 2

Bring a large pot of water to boil for the pasta. Set a bowl large enough to hold the cooked pasta over the pot of heating water and add the sliced garlic, cheese, broken into pieces, and butter. As the water heats, everything will begin to soften and melt.

When the water comes to a boil, remove the bowl and add salt to taste. Add the pasta and give it a stir to separate the pieces. Cook until the pasta is as done as you like it, then scoop it out and add it directly to the bowl with the melted cheese. (Don't worry if all of the cheese hasn't melted—the heat of the pasta will do the rest.) Toss everything together, season with pepper to taste, and serve right away in heated soup plates.

This eccentric Roman pasta is bound to become a classic. It can be made with ingredients from the cupboard, and it has a wonderful mysterious taste. Don't be alarmed by the amount of vodka; the alcohol evaporates quickly to leave the magical ingredients of the sauce.

Pasta with Vodka
(Pasta alla wodka)

Jo Bettoja and Anna Maria Cornetto

SERVES 6

Bring 6 quarts water and 2 tablespoons coarse salt to boil in a large pasta pot. When the water is boiling, add the penne and cook until *al dente*. Meanwhile, warm the bowl in which you intend to serve the pasta.

While the pasta is cooking, prepare the sauce: Melt the butter in a skillet large enough to hold the pasta when cooked. Add the pepper flakes and the vodka and simmer for 2 minutes. Add the tomatoes and cream and simmer for 5 minutes. Add 1 teaspoon coarse salt.

When the pasta is *al dente,* drain well and pour into the skillet with the hot sauce. With the flame on simmer, add the Parmesan and mix thoroughly. Pour into the heated bowl and serve at once.

Coarse salt
1 pound 5 ounces penne
7 tablespoons unsalted butter
½ teaspoon hot red-pepper flakes, or more to taste
1 cup less 2 tablespoons vodka, Polish or Russian
1 scant cup canned Italian plum tomatoes, drained and pureed
1 scant cup heavy cream
1 cup freshly grated Parmesan

Pasta with Eggplant Sauce

(Pasta alle melanzane)

Giuliano Bugialli

2 sweet bell peppers, any color

2 medium Italian eggplants (about 1 pound total)

Coarse salt

1 medium red onion, peeled

1 large clove garlic, peeled

⅓ cup olive oil

½ cup cold water

Salt and freshly ground black pepper

½ teaspoon hot red pepper flakes

1 pound dried short tubular pasta such as rigatoni or penne rigate

This is a delicious, low-fat way to serve eggplant. The dish couldn't be easier to assemble, and if there are any leftovers, it can be extended into an oven casserole. Just add a scattering of plum tomatoes and cubes of fontina or mozzarella cheese and cover the top with bread crumbs that have been tossed in oil.

SERVES 4 TO 6

Clean the peppers, but do not cut into their sides; remove stems, cores, and seeds through the stem end. Cut the peppers into rings less than 1 inch wide, and soak them in a bowl of cold water for 30 minutes. Clean the eggplants and remove their stems; cut them, unpeeled, into 1-inch cubes and soak them in a bowl of cold water with a little coarse salt for 10 minutes. Coarsely chop the onion and garlic together on a board.

Pour the oil into a medium-sized flameproof casserole, add the chopped onion and garlic, then drain the pepper rings and place them on top. Drain and rinse the eggplant cubes very well under cold running water, pat them dry with paper towels, and arrange them over the peppers. Cover the casserole and put it over medium heat: cook for 15 minutes without stirring. Add cold water, salt and pepper to taste, and red pepper flakes, then cover again and cook for 20 minutes more, stirring every so often with a wooden spoon.

Bring a large pot of cold water to a boil, add coarse salt to taste, then add the pasta and cook until *al dente*, for 9 to 12 minutes depending on the brand. Drain the pasta, transfer it to a warmed serving platter, pour the sauce over, mix, and serve.

The perfume of simmering clams, garlic, and lemon is just about irresistible. Ms. Waters suggests trying the recipe with mussels or a mixture of clams and mussels and a hint of saffron.

Clams, Gremolata, and Linguine

Alice Waters

SERVES 4

*W*ash the clams thoroughly. Steam them open in a covered pot with a little chopped onion or shallot, the parsley stems, a sprig of thyme, a bay leaf, and a little white wine. Cook over high heat until they just open; be careful not to overcook or they will toughen. Remove them from the pot, allow to cool, and take them out of their shells. Let the sand settle to the bottom of the juices, and then carefully pour off the liquid through a strainer. Reserve about 1 cup.

To make the gremolata, finely chop the parsley leaves and garlic cloves. Grate the lemon zest very fine and mix the three together.

Combine 1 cup of cream and approximately 1 cup of clam juice (depending on how salty it is) and simmer together. While the pasta is boiling, add the clams and half the gremolata to the sauce. Do not allow the clams to cook any further, just heat through. Add the noodles and toss well. Season with black pepper and serve with the remaining gremolata sprinkled on top.

3 pounds small tender clams (approximately 20 per pound)
Chopped onion or shallot
1 small bunch fresh Italian parsley
1 sprig of fresh thyme
1 bay leaf
White wine
2 or 3 garlic cloves
1 small lemon
1 cup heavy cream
Linguine for 4
Pepper

Pasta with Crabmeat

(Vermicelli ai granchi)

Giuliano Bugialli

4 large garlic cloves, peeled

½ cup olive oil

2½ pounds very ripe, fresh tomatoes
    or 2½ pounds canned tomatoes,
    preferably imported Italian,
    drained

Salt and freshly ground black pepper

1 teaspoon hot red-pepper flakes

Coarse salt

1 pound dried vermicelli or
    spaghetti, preferably imported
    Italian

½ pound lump crabmeat

30 large sprigs of Italian parsley,
    leaves only

This recipe struck us as a special way to serve crabmeat in season. We particularly like the lively contribution of the hot red-pepper flakes.

SERVES 4 TO 6

Coarsely chop the garlic on a board. Place the oil in a medium-sized heavy casserole over medium heat. Add the chopped garlic and sauté for 5 minutes. If fresh tomatoes are used, cut them into pieces. Pass the fresh or canned tomatoes through a food mill, using the disk with the smallest holes, into a bowl. Add the tomatoes to the casserole; season to taste with salt and pepper and add the red-pepper flakes. Simmer for 25 minutes, stirring every so often with a wooden spoon.

Meanwhile, bring a large pot of cold water to a boil. Add coarse salt to taste, then add the pasta and cook until *al dente,* for 9 to 12 minutes depending on the brand. When the tomato sauce is ready, add the crabmeat and simmer for 5 minutes more. Coarsely chop the parsley. Drain the pasta and transfer to a large, warmed serving platter; pour the sauce over and toss very well. Sprinkle the parsley over, toss again, and serve immediately.

Accompaniments

VEGETABLES

Asparagus Poêlé

Baked Red Beets

Broccoli Smothered in Garlic Oil

Shredded Brussels Sprouts

Sweet and Sour Red Cabbage

Wondrous Carrots

Cauliflower with Raisins and Pine Nuts

Pureed Celery Root with Apples

Corn Fritters

Early Summer Fresh Corn Pudding

Sweet and Sour Eggplant

Baked Eggplant

Sautéed Fennel with Lemon

Roasted Garlic

Braised Garlic and String Beans

Oven-roasted Green Beans

Stir-fried Green Beans

Tawny Mushroom Caps

Sautéed–Braised Chanterelles

Big Baked Onions

Roasted Onions with Sage

Pureed Parsnips

Peas and Cucumber in Dill

Slivered Snow Peas and Toasted
   Almonds

Baked Potatoes

Stuffed Baked Potatoes

Twice-baked Sweet Potatoes

Mashed Potatoes

Mashed Sweet Potatoes

Roasted Potatoes

Oven-fried Sweet Potatoes

Sautéed Potatoes

Double Bliss Potatoes

Savory Sweet Potatoes with Shiitakes

Potato Gratin

Baked Peppers, Potatoes, and Onions

Herbed New Potatoes with Vermouth

Hot Devil Potatoes
Potato Cakes
Red Radishes Sautéed with Vinegar
Skillet Scallions
Spinach and Pear Puree
Slow-baked Tomatoes
Sautéed Cherry Tomatoes
Turnips à la Comtesse
Stir-fried Zucchini with Sesame Seeds
Zucchini Stuffed with Corn and Cheese

BEANS AND GRAINS

Ten-minute Black Beans with Tomatoes
   and Coriander
Lentil Puree
Steamed Rice
Pilaf
Fried Rice
Spinach Pilaf

Saffron Risotto
Hominy
Cheese Grits
Firm Polenta
Spoon Bread
Basic Couscous

*T*raditionally accompaniments have been considered dull necessities, a combination of vitamins and ballast that justifies dessert. But we think side dishes have become the most interesting part of today's meals. The American way with vegetables has changed entirely in the last ten years, as our devotion to meat has waned and the availability of produce has increased considerably.

We often build an entire menu around what's in season; except for a few fish and shellfish, main course choices are virtually always in season—but not asparagus, or great tomatoes, or acorn squash. A fat purse will buy almost anything out of season, anything but great taste. An added advantage of serving produce in season is that it's already at its best, and you'll have much less to do in the kitchen.

Then there are the sustaining side dishes of the meal, its ballast, and more often than not, they take the role of comfort food as well. They're also particularly homey dishes—no restaurant can produce as great a baked potato as you can in your own kitchen. We're as nostalgic about these foods as everyone else, but we also like to come up with some surprises. There are a lot of interesting options available these days: couscous, polenta, orzo, and all sorts of unusual rices and noodles.

A general air of festivity surrounds a meal with lots of accompaniments—one of the great secrets of the success of Thanksgiving. Even one additional side dish will be received with great pleasure. If you're serving a buffet, extra side dishes also provide choices for vegetarians or guests on special diets. Try to serve at least one low-fat accompaniment. Plan the contrasts of color and texture as well as taste. And, particularly if you're serving a buffet, remember that a number of side dishes can be served at room temperature.

Asparagus Poêlé

Jasper White

1 pound medium asparagus, peeled
Salt and freshly ground pepper
4 tablespoons unsalted butter

This has to be the easiest—and possibly the best—way to cook asparagus. There's no fussing, no draining, and all the juices stay in the spears, ready to release their springlike perfume when you uncover the dish at the table. But don't use this method with pencil-thin asparagus; it won't work.

SERVES 4

Preheat the oven to 350°. Line up the asparagus in a covered casserole or earthenware dish that will hold all of them in no more than 2 layers. Season lightly with salt and pepper and dot with butter. Add 2 tablespoons water and cover tightly.

Place in the preheated oven. For medium asparagus allow 17 minutes; for larger ones, 20 minutes. Bring to the table and uncover.

Serving Suggestions: Asparagus has a real affinity for ham, lamb, and salmon. Serve it with Salmon Slices with Walnut or Hazelnut Vinaigrette (page 56) or Wild Mushroom Meat Loaf (page 92).

Tips:
Choose spears about half an inch in diameter, with tightly closed tips and no more than an inch of white at the base; trim the stems by snapping them off wherever they break naturally with slight pressure.

You may want to peel the asparagus; we think it improves both the appearance and the taste and is worth the few minutes it takes to flick off the tough outer skin with a vegetable peeler.

Wrap peeled asparagus in damp paper towels and store them in the refrigerator if you do them ahead of time.

Store asparagus up to 4 days in the refrigerator crisper, rolling them in damp paper towels and then sealing them in a plastic bag.

Variations:

Serve the asparagus with freshly shaved or grated Parmesan. Bake as in the recipe, add a little cheese, and drizzle the baking juices over the top or add extra butter. Place the dish under the broiler to slightly melt and brown the cheese.

From Edward Giobbi: Use 3 tablespoons olive oil instead of butter and 2 tablespoons dried mint (or ½ cup minced fresh mint); bake at 400° for 12 to 15 minutes in a dish covered with foil.

From Elisabeth Luard: Paint big spears with olive oil, add salt and pepper, then grill the asparagus under the broiler just until the spears begin to turn golden on each side. Serve hot or at room temperature with a fresh herb sauce made by blending 1 cup mint, parsley, basil, watercress, or chives (or a combination) with 1 garlic clove, ⅓ cup olive oil, 2 tablespoons fresh lemon juice, and salt to taste.

Serve chilled asparagus with a simple mustard vinaigrette or with light mayonnaise cut with yogurt and seasoned with minced fresh mint and grated orange or lemon zest.

From Roy Andries de Groot comes an unusual combination: Make a sauce by melting ¼ pound (1 stick) butter in a small saucepan; when it is quite hot but not yet brown, add ¼ cup ground pecans. Stir for a few seconds until they just turn color, then throw in, all at once, 1 teaspoon tarragon vinegar. There will be a violent hissing and frothing. Stir once more and spoon immediately over the asparagus. Makes enough for 6 servings.

Baked Red Beets

(Rape rosse al forno)

Marcella Hazan

1 bunch fresh beets, about 4 to
    6 beets, depending on size
Salt
Olive oil
Wine vinegar

For some unfathomable reason, people go to all sorts of trouble boiling and steaming beets when the most delicious way to cook them is also the easiest—roasting them in foil in the oven. This process concentrates their flavor to an intense, mouth-filling sweetness that is a revelation to anyone tasting them for the first time.

SERVES 4

Cut off the tops of the beets at the base of the stems, but do not discard. Trim the root ends of the beets.

Rinse the beets in cold water. Wrap them all together in aluminum foil, making sure it is very tightly sealed.

Put them on the upper rack of the oven and turn the thermostat to 400°. They should be done in about 1½ to 2 hours, depending on their size. To test them, run a fork into them; they should be tender but firm. When done, remove them from the oven and from the foil.

While they are still warm but cool enough to handle, pull away the blackish skin around them. Cut them into thin slices.

When ready to serve, season them with salt, olive oil, and good red-wine vinegar. They can be served while still slightly warm or at room temperature. They are best the day they are done and not refrigerated. But if necessary they can be prepared a day or two ahead of time and kept peeled but whole in plastic wrap in the refrigerator. Bring them to room temperature well before serving.

Serving Suggestions: Serve with Beef Braised in Coffee (page 90) or Sicilian Meatballs with Raisins and Pine Nuts (page 106).

Tips:

Add a little water to the foil package or reduce the cooking temperature to 300° if you prefer a milder, juicier beet (high-temperature roasting results in an intense, slightly caramelized flavor). Small beets will be done in 1 hour.

Test the beets with a sharp knife rather than a fork or by pressing with your thumb. They are done when the knife slides in easily or when the pressure of your thumb loosens the skin.

If the beet greens are pretty and fresh-looking, you're in great luck: Cook them like spinach or blanch them and toss them with oil and lemon juice for a wonderful warm salad. If the leaves are large, devein them by pulling the stem back across the leaf to remove the tough and fibrous strings.

Variations:

Dress the beets with balsamic vinegar and a blend of walnut and olive oils.

Serve cold sliced beets with a dollop of sour cream mixed with lots of freshly minced dill.

Broccoli Smothered in Garlic Oil

(Hare gobhi ki sabzi)

Julie Sahni

1 bunch broccoli (about 1½ pounds)
3 tablespoons light vegetable oil
8 to 10 garlic cloves, peeled
⅓ teaspoon turmeric
1 teaspoon kosher salt

Broccoli is such a virtuous vegetable that we're always looking for interesting new ways to prepare it. This elegant, subtle dish is a standout that's particularly good with lamb.

SERVES 4 TO 6

Cut broccoli into spears, leaving long stems attached to the florets. Peel the stems carefully—they break easily. Rinse the spears under running cold water. Leave them for 5 minutes to drain.

Heat the oil over medium-high heat in a frying pan large enough to accommodate the broccoli in a single layer. When the oil is hot, add garlic, and sauté, turning and tossing until it turns golden (about 1 to 2 minutes). Add turmeric and immediately follow it with the broccoli. Spread the broccoli so that it lies in one layer. Let it sizzle undisturbed for 1 minute, then sprinkle on the salt. Turn the broccoli carefully with a flat spatula or a pair of tongs, and sauté for an additional minute.

Reduce heat and cook, covered, until the broccoli is cooked but still crisp and dark green (about 8 to 10 minutes). Uncover and continue cooking until all the moisture evaporates and the broccoli spears are glazed with garlic oil (about 3 to 5 minutes). Check for salt and serve immediately.

Tips:
Rather than skip the peeling step, to hurry this dish along use just the florets, and you'll save at least 5 minutes.

Cut the broccoli pieces roughly the same size so they'll cook evenly.

It's amazing what happens to Brussels sprouts when you take them apart before you cook them. You can peel them leaf by leaf, a somewhat laborious operation, or simply shred them, as in this recipe. Either way, you get a sweet, succulent vegetable.

Shredded Brussels Sprouts

Susan Feniger and Mary Sue Milliken

SERVES 6 TO 8

1½ pounds Brussels sprouts
4 tablespoons unsalted butter
½ teaspoon salt
¼ teaspoon white pepper
2 teaspoons water
Juice of ½ lime

*S*oak whole sprouts in a large bowl of cold salted water to clean, then trim and discard ends and any bitter outer leaves. Cut each in half lengthwise, then slice thinly across width.

Melt butter in a large skillet over medium-high heat. Sauté sprouts with salt and pepper until they start to brown. Add water and cook until barely limp, about 4 minutes. (The water changes the action from sautéing to steaming.) Stir in lime juice and serve immediately.

Serving Suggestions: Serve the sprouts with Pork Chops (page 104) or Church-Supper Ham Loaf (page 110). They'd also be good with Pork Slices with Prunes (page 102).

Tip: Taste the lime juice and adjust the quantity to the sweetness of the fruit since this recipe comes from California, where citrus is often riper and sweeter than it is in other parts of the country.

Sweet and Sour Red Cabbage

Susan Feniger and Mary Sue Milliken

1 large head red cabbage
2 large onions, thinly sliced
½ cup granulated sugar
1 cup red-wine vinegar
1 tablespoon caraway seeds
1 bay leaf
1½ teaspoons salt
¼ teaspoon pepper
½ cup rendered duck fat, preferably,
   or clarified butter

This cabbage dish is more of a condiment than an accompaniment. It's very flexible: It tastes even better made days ahead of time; it can be served hot or cold; and it goes with all kinds of dishes, from Thanksgiving fare to sandwiches.

SERVES 10 TO 12

Cut cabbage in quarters, core, and finely julienne. Combine all ingredients, except the fat, in a large bowl. Stir to blend.

Heat fat in a large heavy skillet or Dutch oven over moderate heat. Add cabbage mixture and reduce heat to a simmer. Cover and cook, stirring occasionally, until cabbage is tender, about 1 hour. Serve hot or cold. Sweet and sour cabbage may be stored in refrigerator up to 5 days and may also be reheated.

Serving Suggestions: Serve with roast pork (pages 97–101) or even liver. Tuck it into robust sandwiches or use it to garnish pâtés, terrines, or smoked fish.

Tips: Cook the red cabbage in the microwave; it shouldn't take more than 15 or 20 minutes, but be sure to stir at 5-minute intervals.

Variations: Substitute bacon fat for the clarified butter and brown sugar for the white. If you're not a vinegar fan, substitute red wine for the vinegar; slice a tart apple into the cabbage before cooking.

Wondrous Carrots

Camille Glenn

This simple carrot dish is inexplicably delicious. Ms. Glenn likes these carrots so much she thinks they ought to be served alone, the better to savor them. We agree, but we also like them mixed with, of all things, the Brussels sprouts on page 139; they're wonderful together.

SERVES 2

2 cups sliced fresh carrots
3 tablespoons unsalted butter
1½ teaspoons sugar, or to taste
2 tablespoons cognac or brandy, or
    more to taste
Salt to taste (very little)
Chopped fresh parsley, for garnish

Drop the carrots into boiling water to barely cover. Don't add salt. Simmer, uncovered, until just tender, 15 to 17 minutes. The carrots should not get too soft, but they should lose a measure of their crispness.

Drain the carrots if the water has not boiled away. Add the butter, sugar, and cognac or brandy. Toss over low heat just a few seconds for the cognac to mellow. Add very little salt, if any, and garnish with parsley.

Serving Suggestions: Serve with Rack of Lamb with Anise and Sweet Garlic (page 116) or Ham Baked in Cola (page 107).

Tips:
Camille Glenn says never add salt to carrots before they're finished cooking; use a little sugar instead.

Blanch carrots ahead of time to cut down the final cooking time by cooking them briefly and cooling them in iced water; drain well and store in the refrigerator. You can also blanch carrots in the microwave.

Variations:
Use bourbon instead of brandy or omit the sugar and substitute Triple Sec or Grand Marnier.

Omit the alcohol and glaze the carrots in butter and sugar.

Substitute the peeled and rounded carrot bits that look like baby carrots; they are ready to cook and take only 2 minutes in the microwave.

Cauliflower with Raisins and Pine Nuts

(Cavolfiore con l'uvetta e i pignoli)

Marcella Hazan

1 ounce seedless raisins
1 young head cauliflower (about 1½ pounds)
⅓ cup extra virgin olive oil
2 teaspoons finely chopped garlic
1 ounce pine nuts
Salt
Black pepper in a grinder
2 tablespoons chopped parsley

An unusual way to prepare the often maligned cauliflower. The southern Italian seasonings are perfect for cauliflower.

SERVES 4 TO 6

Soak the raisins in water for 15 to 20 minutes.

Trim the cauliflower of all its outer leaves except for the tender, almost totally white ones. Drop it into 4 quarts of boiling water. After the water returns to a boil, cook for 6 to 7 minutes until it is halfway done, that is, until you feel resistance when pricking it with a fork. Drain it and cut it into 1½-inch pieces.

When the raisins have finished soaking, drain them and squeeze them gently in your hands to force off excess liquid.

Choose a lidded sauté pan that can subsequently accommodate all the cauliflower pieces without overlapping. Put in the oil and the garlic and turn on the heat to medium without covering the pan.

When the garlic becomes colored a pale gold, add the cauliflower, raisins, pine nuts, salt, generous grindings of pepper. Cover the pan and turn down the heat to low. Cook for 8 to 10 minutes or more, stirring from time to time, until the cauliflower feels tender when tested with a fork. Sprinkle on the chopped parsley and serve hot.

Serving Suggestions: Serve with Veal Shanks (page 95) or Garlicky Baked Chicken Pieces (page 66).

Tips:
Use the microwave for the initial blanching.

Save some of the blanched cauliflower for one of the variations.

Note: Buy cauliflower that's dazzlingly white, with no brown spots, and use it as soon as you can. The lovely mild taste depends on freshness; cauliflower that's been stored either at home or in the market develops that strong cabbagey flavor many people find unpleasant.

Variations:
Sauté the blanched cauliflower in garlic and oil; toss in a few capers. Stop there or add sweet red pepper strips or drained Italian plum tomatoes.

Sauté the blanched cauliflower in butter; sprinkle with toasted sliced almonds.

Top the fully cooked cauliflower with fine bread crumbs mixed with melted butter, minced parsley, and chives.

Pureed Celery Root with Apples

(Purée de céleri-rave aux pommes)

Paula Wolfert after Michel Guérard

1 pound celery root
1 quart milk
¾ pound Delicious apples
2 to 3 tablespoons heavy cream
Salt and pepper

This incredibly delicious puree, light, silky, and somewhat mysterious in flavor, can be made several hours ahead and reheated perfectly.

SERVES 4 TO 6

Peel celery root and cut into chunks using a stainless steel knife. In a noncorrodible saucepan, simmer, covered with milk, 10 minutes.

Meanwhile peel, core, and quarter the apples. Add to the celery and cook together 10 minutes, or until celery root is tender. Drain.

Puree celery root and apple quarters in batches in food processor until smooth. Add the cream if necessary to loosen the mixture. Season with salt and pepper to taste. For a perfectly textured puree, push the pureed mixture through a fine wire sieve.

Serving Suggestions: Serve with roast pork, duck, or ham. This dish would also be good with Rolled Stuffed Turkey Cutlets (page 81). The puree is elegant enough to serve at a holiday meal.

Tips:
To peel a celery root, slice off the top and bottom, removing the roots and the tuft of leaves; score the skin, as you would an orange, and pull it right off.

Drop peeled celery root immediately into water acidulated with lemon juice or vinegar.

Use the microwave to cook a celery root without peeling; pierce the skin to keep it from bursting and cook on high until soft (10 minutes for 1 pound of celery root).

Corn Fritters

Margaret Fox

Corn fritters are one of those old-fashioned American grand-mothers' dishes that we tend to forget about. These are extremely good and very easy to make, and can be made virtually fat-free. Margaret Fox likes them made with corn that's just picked; they're also very good—but different—made with older corn. And we even like them in winter, made with creamed corn. Serve them with sour cream, or Mexican tomato and jalapeño salsa, or with maple syrup or honey.

MAKES ABOUT 2 DOZEN FRITTERS

Mix all ingredients together. Drop the batter by generous tablespoon into a very lightly greased nonstick pan. Cook like pancakes, about 1 minute each side, turning once when lightly brown.

2 cups freshly grated corn
2 eggs, lightly beaten
2 tablespoons flour
1 teaspoon baking powder
1 teaspoon salt
Ground pepper

Serving Suggestions: Serve with barbecued spareribs, Ham Steaks (page 108), Orange-spiced Chicken Wings (page 64), or Catfish Baked with Cheese (page 62).

Tips:
Stir in a bit more flour, the less the better, if you have trouble turning the fritters; they are very delicate.

Use oil instead of butter to grease the pan; you may not need any with a nonstick pan.

Variations:

Make cheese fritters by dotting the uncooked tops with tiny dice of fontina, Cheddar, or Monterey Jack. These would be perfect with a grilled skirt steak smothered in roasted sweet peppers.

Make the fritters with the same quantity of canned creamed corn in winter. Double the amount of flour and taste the mixture before you add salt.

Early Summer Fresh Corn Pudding

Camille Glenn

6 ears tender fresh corn
3 eggs, beaten
1 cup heavy cream
⅓ cup milk
1 teaspoon salt
1 tablespoon sugar

This is the best corn pudding we've ever eaten, even when made in February with frozen shoepeg corn. (Hanover is a good brand.) It's very simple and very pretty, and when you slice through the golden top, it releases a nostalgic Mom's-Sunday-supper aroma.

SERVES 6

Preheat the oven to 350°.

Cut the corn from the cob and scrape the cobs well to extract the milk. You should have 2 cups of corn.

In a large bowl, mix the eggs, cream, and milk. Add the salt, sugar, and corn.

Pour the mixture into a buttered shallow casserole or heatproof glass dish. Place in a shallow pan of warm water and bake until a knife inserted in the center comes out clean, about 1 hour.

Serving Suggestions: Serve the pudding with Ham Baked in Cola (page 107) or Ham Steaks (page 108), or with a simple roast chicken (pages 71 and 72) and green salad.

Tip: Ms. Glenn has built in the secret of avoiding curdling in corn puddings: Cook them in shallow 1½-quart heatproof glass dishes. Other recipes add a lot of extra flour to compensate for the standard deep American casserole dishes, which produce a watery, curdled pudding. If that's the only kind you've ever tasted, this dish will be a revelation.

Variations:

Sprinkle freshly grated nutmeg and snipped fresh chives on top if you use frozen corn.

Substitute frozen shoepeg corn for the fresh corn. Thaw 2 cups kernels and process with ¼ cup milk to get 2 cups of corn.

Some recipes, even those with no surprises like this one, are just plain winners. It's all in the balance and contrast of ingredients. If you love eggplant, you'll love this dish.

Sweet and Sour Eggplant

Susan Feniger and Mary Sue Milliken

SERVES 6

Trim ends of eggplants. Cut across width into ¼-inch slices, leaving skins on. (If you are using regular eggplants, cut into quarters lengthwise before slicing.) Place in a colander, sprinkle with coarse salt, and let sweat 30 minutes. Pat dry with paper towels.

Heat oil in a large skillet over high heat. Sauté eggplant in batches until lightly brown, about 1 minute per side. Set aside to drain on paper towels.

In same pan, sauté onions until golden. Reduce heat, add garlic, and cook just long enough to release its aroma. Add tomato paste and cook 2 minutes. Stir in

3½ pounds eggplant, preferably Japanese
1 tablespoon coarse salt
1 cup olive oil
2 large onions, diced
2 tablespoons pureed garlic
½ cup red-wine vinegar
1½ tablespoons tomato paste
⅓ cup capers with juice
½ cup brown sugar
Salt and Tabasco to taste

remaining ingredients. Continue cooking another 3 minutes. Taste to adjust seasonings. Serve immediately or chill a minimum of 2 hours or up to 2 days.

Serving Suggestions: Serve with Pork Tenderloin (page 104), Spicy Skirt Steak with Cinnamon (page 89), or Veal Shanks (page 95).

Tip: Skip the step of sweating the eggplant if you're using Japanese eggplants, to make this a super-fast recipe. Though they may absorb more oil initially, they'll release it after they're cooked; drain them.

Baked Eggplant (Melanzane al forno)

Jo Bettoja and Anna Maria Cornetto

2 pounds large round eggplant (of the
    same size, if possible), cut into
    ½-inch slices
Coarse salt
½ cup extra virgin olive oil
2 tablespoons fresh lemon juice
1 teaspoon dried oregano, or more to
    taste
Freshly ground black pepper to taste

This simple eggplant dish is extraordinarily good, but that's only one of its virtues. Because it doesn't need to be refrigerated, it's a good choice for company buffets when refrigerator space is at a premium. And because the flavor only improves with age, you can make it well ahead of time.

SERVES 6

Layer the eggplant slices in a colander, salting each layer. Leave for 1 hour. Rinse and pat dry.

Preheat the oven to 425°.

Pour half the oil into a 15 × 12-inch roasting pan or pizza pan. Dip half the eggplant slices in the oil, coating both sides, and bake for 10 minutes. Remove the pan from the oven, turn the slices over, and cook for about 10 minutes more.

Remove the slices to a platter, pour over half the lemon juice, sprinkle on ½ teaspoon oregano, and salt and pepper the slices.

Put the rest of the oil into the pan and repeat the process with the rest of the eggplant. Serve at room temperature.

Serving Suggestions: Serve with Great Roast Chicken (pages 71 and 72) with a light cream pan sauce (page 75) or a roasted chicken or turkey breast (page 79) seasoned under the skin with black olive paste (page 74).

Tips:

Obviously you can use two pans at once or one very large pan and save yourself 20 minutes. You can also brush the eggplant slices with the olive oil to cut down on the oil.

Search out imported Greek, Italian, or Mexican oregano, which has an intense aromatic quality; crush the oregano between your fingers when you sprinkle it over the eggplant.

Buy firm and unblemished eggplant that feels heavy in your hand (generally speaking, long, thin eggplant is less pulpy than the voluptuous still-life variety); thin-skinned Italian eggplant is worth the extra price. If your eggplant has a thick skin, it's best to peel it for this recipe.

Eggplant doesn't keep well either in the market or at home; buy it shortly before you cook it.

From Elizabeth Schneider: Don't salt and sweat the eggplant first. We are divided about this, so try it and see what you think—you could save yourself hours of kitchen time.

From Jo Bettoja: Instead of salting and sweating, soak sliced eggplant for at least 12 hours in heavily salted cold water; you don't even have to dry it unless you're planning to fry the eggplant, in which case it does need to be really dry.

Variation: If you have leftovers, cut the eggplant into strips and combine with some quickly sautéed seeded fresh tomatoes, a cupped palm full of chopped fresh herbs, and salt and pepper. Cook very briefly and spoon over pasta.

Sautéed Fennel with Lemon

Elizabeth Schneider

2 medium fennel bulbs (with tiny top
    stalks, or very few), about 1½
    pounds
2 tablespoons olive oil or butter
¼ teaspoon salt, or to taste
½ to 1 teaspoon finely grated lemon
    zest
Pepper to taste

We like the subtle anise taste of fennel, and the simple lemon zest seasoning here provides the right astringent touch.

SERVES 3

Trim and reserve the fennel leaves and cut off and reserve top stalks, if any. Quarter each bulb lengthwise; cut each quarter crosswise in very thin slivers. Mince 1 tablespoon of the fine leaves.

Heat oil in large, heavy skillet; toss fennel slices to coat. Add salt. Continue tossing frequently over moderate heat, until tender—about 10 minutes.

Toss with lemon zest and pepper to taste. Sprinkle with minced tops.

Serving Suggestions: Serve with any fish fillets, salmon steak, Grilled Swordfish with Mustard (page 58), or Salmon Slices with Walnut or Hazelnut Vinaigrette (page 56).

Note: Fennel isn't always easy to find in the market, but it's worth asking your greengrocer to stock it. Fennel season runs from fall to early spring with peak abundance around the holidays.

Variations:
Add sautéed peppers, mushrooms, or snow peas—or all of them together.

Toss raw fennel slices with orange slices, red onion slices, and black olives. Dress the salad with olive oil and lemon juice.

EDITOR'S KITCHEN

There are so many good uses for roasted garlic that we try to keep some in the refrigerator at all times. Whenever you use your oven, put a couple of heads of garlic in to roast, and then they'll be waiting for you when culinary imagination strikes.

Roasted Garlic

FOR EACH GARLIC HEAD

Preheat the oven to 325°. Pull off any loose, papery peel from the garlic head. With a very sharp knife, slice off just enough of the top to expose the cloves. (If you notice any green sprouts in the center of the garlic cloves, use that head for another purpose—sprouted garlic tends to be bitter and will not roast to a sweet puree.) Stand the garlic head on a piece of heavy foil, drizzle a little olive oil over the exposed top, and sprinkle with salt and pepper. Fold the foil tightly around the garlic and place the package in the oven for 1 hour. When ready to use, squeeze the butter-soft cloves out of their papery casing from the bottom, the way you squeeze toothpaste out of the tube. Store unused or partially used heads in the refrigerator, well covered.

Tips:
Add the roasted garlic to salad dressings, mayonnaise, soft butter for croustades, and pan drippings before deglazing.

Smooth it into cream reductions for topping pasta, chicken breasts, or fish fillets.

Squeeze it onto oiled toast and float the toast on top of soup.

Variations:
Add a sprig of fresh thyme or rosemary to the package, especially if you plan to use whole heads of garlic as an accompaniment to a roast or on crusty bread.

Squeeze out 6 whole roasted heads of garlic into ¼ cup mild olive oil. Add 2 rounded tablespoons of bottled mayonnaise and pulse in the food processor until smooth and creamy. (This may take longer than you expect.) The result is a fantastic, unctuous concentrate that you can keep in the refrigerator for seasoning, sauces, and salad dressings—anytime a smooth, sweet, intense garlic flavor would be appreciated.

Fresh green beans with succulent golden garlic and sage—what could be better?

Braised Garlic and String Beans

Bert Greene

SERVES 4

Cook the string beans in boiling salted water until crisp-tender, about 1½ to 2 minutes. Rinse under cold running water until cool. Drain.

Melt the butter in a large skillet over low heat. Add the garlic cloves and cook, covered, until lightly golden and soft, 20 to 25 minutes. Do not let the butter burn. Remove the cover and mash the garlic with a fork until well mixed with the butter.

Add the beans to the skillet; toss over medium heat until warmed through. Add the sage, parsley, and salt and pepper to taste.

Serving Suggestions: Serve with Succulent Pork Roast with Fennel (page 99), Catfish Baked with Cheese (page 62), or Ham Steaks (page 108).

Tips:

You don't have to pinch off the beans' tails—just the tips—unless they're very tough.

Be careful not to overcook the beans—5 minutes is about the maximum any bean could need.

Use the microwave to precook the beans up to 1 or 2 days ahead of time and store them, covered, in the refrigerator to save time when ready to prepare the dish.

1 pound tender young string beans, trimmed (cut larger beans French-style)
3 tablespoons unsalted butter
4 to 5 large garlic cloves
1 teaspoon chopped fresh sage or a pinch of dried sage
1 tablespoon chopped fresh parsley
Salt and freshly ground black pepper

To cut about 25 minutes from the recipe, substitute Roasted Garlic (page 151) for the fresh garlic, squeezing it into the butter and mashing thoroughly with a fork.

Variation: Substitute snipped fresh dill or chives for the sage.

EDITORS' KITCHEN

Oven-roasted Green Beans

Another great string-beans-and-garlic routine involves oven-roasting the beans, a particularly good trick for beans that aren't tender.

SERVES 4

For 1 pound of beans, smash up 3 or 4 garlic cloves and add them to ¼ cup olive oil with some fresh or dried herbs, such as rosemary, thyme or lemon thyme, or marjoram. Set aside to infuse for several hours. When you're ready to cook the trimmed beans, remove the garlic cloves, which might burn in the hot oven, and pour the flavored oil over the beans. Add salt and pepper to taste and toss the beans thoroughly with the oil. Arrange the beans so they aren't overlapping in a shallow pan and roast them at 450° for 15 minutes, stirring them once or twice during the cooking.

Variation: Use light sesame oil and a little soy sauce with the garlic instead of olive oil and herbs; scatter toasted sesame seeds over the cooked beans.

Stir-fried Green Beans

Irene Kuo

This simplified version of a curiously delicious gingered recipe has no ginger taste, just the subtle aroma of garlic. Irene Kuo explains that the ginger simply eliminates the faint grassy taste of lightly cooked green beans.

SERVES 3 TO 4

1 pound fresh green beans, trimmed
    and washed
2 tablespoons oil
2 medium garlic cloves, lightly
    smashed and peeled
2 quarter-size slices peeled ginger
1 to 1½ teaspoons salt, to taste
¼ cup chicken stock or water
2 teaspoons sesame oil (optional)

*B*reak the beans in two and dry them thoroughly so that they will not splatter in the hot oil.

Place a wok or sauté pan over high heat, add the oil, swirl, and heat about 30 seconds. Lower heat to medium and toss in the garlic and ginger; press them against the pan for a few seconds. Be careful not to let them burn; if you do, throw them out, along with the oil, and start over.

Turn the heat high and scatter in the green beans. Stir and toss rapidly until every piece is covered with oil and the color has deepened to bright green.

Sprinkle in the salt, toss, and pour in the liquid. Turn heat to medium-low, even out the beans in the pan, cover, and let them steam-cook for about 4 minutes, or until the liquid is almost evaporated.

Remove the cover and stir and flip the beans until the liquid is completely gone. Taste and adjust salt if necessary. If the beans are still a little too hard, add a spoonful of liquid and continue to stir until it disappears. The beans should have some crunch.

Add the sesame oil, if using, and toss, then turn the beans out onto a hot serving dish. Remove the garlic and ginger if you wish.

Serving Suggestions: Serve with Shrimp with Cashew Nuts (page 49) or Braised Chicken Thighs with Spicy Tomato and Ginger Sauce (page 70).

Tip: Smash the garlic cloves with the flat side of a cleaver or wide chef's knife; the peel will slip off easily.

Variations: Add peeled fresh water chestnuts to this stir-fry—or drained canned ones in a pinch; they are sweet and crunchy. They are nearly always available in Asian markets and in the supermarket on occasion.

Tawny Mushroom Caps

Abby Mandel

1 pound large, uniformly sized
   mushrooms
3 tablespoons light-tasting olive oil
1½ tablespoons balsamic vinegar
1½ teaspoons honey
2 tablespoons tawny port
½ teaspoon salt

These mushrooms taste heavenly, and their rich bronze glaze makes them a lovely main course garnish. They also make a fine hot canapé, particularly with a crock of Roquefort and walnut pâté.

SERVES 3 TO 4

Brush the mushrooms or wipe them with a dampened paper towel to remove the dirt. Trim the stems flush with the bottom of the caps. Save stems for another use, if desired.

Put the oil, vinegar, honey, port, and salt in a 10-inch skillet. Cook over high heat until the mixture begins to sizzle, about 3 minutes. Add the mushrooms, rounded side down. Cook, shaking the pan occasionally, until the mushrooms are tender and the liquid has cooked down to a rich syrup that coats them with a thin film. This takes 8 to 10 minutes, depending on the size of the mushrooms.

Serving Suggestions: Serve with a sautéed or grilled steak or Rack of Lamb with Anise and Sweet Garlic (page 116).

Tip: Prepare the mushrooms a day in advance. To reheat, cook gently until they are warmed through, about 5 minutes. Or reheat them, with their liquid, in the microwave on high for 1½ minutes.

Note: Use cremini mushrooms, which are tastier than the cultivated whites, if you can find them. They also deepen the color of the honey and balsamic vinegar gilding.

Sautéed–Braised Chanterelles

Elizabeth Schneider

This wild-mushroom braise is wildly expensive unless you have a woodland source for chanterelles. But the luxury of it puts this recipe into the special-occasion category; it's a perfect choice for a celebration.

SERVES 4

Trim off base tips from chanterelles. Leave mushrooms whole, if tiny, or cut large ones into bite-size pieces.

Heat butter in a large skillet; stir in mushrooms and sauté over moderate heat until barely softened. Add stock and cook over high heat until most liquid has been absorbed. Add wine and toss until almost evaporated. Season and serve with herbs, if desired.

Serving Suggestions: Serve with roast chicken (pages 71 and 72), Cornish hens (page 77), or Veal Scallops with Fennel (page 93). Or offer the mushrooms as a first course at a company dinner, mounded on a piece of freshly toasted French bread; you will have enough for 6 servings.

1 pound chanterelles, cleaned, as needed
2 to 3 tablespoons butter
About 1 cup veal or chicken stock
About ⅓ cup dry white wine or ¼ cup dry vermouth
Salt and pepper to taste
Small amount of minced parsley and/or chives (optional)

Variations:

Prepare a mixed variety of mushrooms, including the less expensive cremini mushrooms and shiitake.

Use small white cultivated mushrooms as a fill and add some wild-mushroom powder, which is now available in specialty markets.

Omit the wine for a different, less diffuse flavor.

Big Baked Onions

Julia Child

1 3-inch onion
About 1 tablespoon butter or sour
   cream

Talk about easy—these onions baked in their skins are just about perfect. A platter of these rustic-looking onions, garnished with sprigs of fresh herbs, is a handsome addition to a buffet table.

FOR EACH SERVING

Preheat the oven to 400° and place the onions root side down (pick onions that will stand up straight) on a baking sheet lined with foil. Set them in the middle level of the oven and bake until they are definitely soft throughout when pressed and when pricked deeply with a small knife or skewer.

Keep warm until ready to serve. At serving time, slit the tops and place a pat of butter or a spoonful of sour cream in each. To eat them, scoop the warm flesh out of the surrounding skin.

Serving Suggestions: Serve with beef, lamb, pork, or chicken. Onions complement almost any main dish except the most delicate fish. These are best suited to simple grilled or roasted meat.

Variation: Charcoal-grill the onions: Microwave them for 15 to 20 minutes (prick them first so they won't burst) or bake them until thoroughly cooked, then slice off the tops just enough to expose the flesh of the onion. Rub the whole onion with oil and place on the grill, cut end down, then turn on the side. A few minutes will char the skins attractively, and a slight smoky taste will permeate the flesh of the onion.

Roasted Onions with Sage

Deborah Madison

2 pounds red or yellow onions
Salt
2 to 4 tablespoons virgin olive oil
1 dozen fresh sage leaves or 1 teaspoon dried sage
1 teaspoon coarsely ground pepper
2 tablespoons balsamic vinegar
Butter or oil for baking dish
Finely chopped parsley

This recipe is so simple and straightforward that it's hard to believe the result is so amazingly good. Both red and yellow onions can be used here.

SERVES 4 TO 6

*P*reheat the oven to 375°. Peel the onions and slice them into rounds about ½ inch or more thick. Separate the rings, then toss them with salt, olive oil, sage, pepper, and vinegar. Lightly butter or oil a large gratin dish, add the seasoned onions, cover with foil, and bake for 30 minutes. Remove the foil, give the onions a stir, cover, and return the dish to the oven for 15 minutes. They should be starting to brown all over. Stir again and return to the oven, uncovered, 15 minutes more or until the juices reduce to a syrup and the onions are done. Serve heaped in a bowl with some finely chopped parsley.

Serving Suggestions: Serve with grilled steak, Pork Chops (page 104), Pork Tenderloin (page 104), or

Great Roast Chicken (pages 71 and 72). Or smother a poached chicken breast with the onions or dress up a hamburger or baked potato. Ms. Madison likes to pile the onions on grilled bread brushed with walnut oil and top them with thin shavings of Parmesan cheese.

Tips:
Start the onions in the microwave in an ovenproof glass dish, covered with plastic wrap. Cook them on high until soft, uncover, and transfer to the preheated oven to brown and glaze.

Fix the onions when you have something else cooking in the oven and store them in the refrigerator to use later.

Variations:
Substitute thyme for sage.

Mix in some slivered sun-dried tomatoes and broccoli—or cauliflower, as Madison suggests—florets and use the chopped onions as a sauce for pasta.

Pureed Parsnips

James Beard

Madeira brings out the natural sweetness of parsnips. This was one of James Beard's favorite vegetable dishes. It's particularly appropriate for a holiday dinner.

SERVES 6 TO 8

Peel cooked parsnips and puree them in a food processor or by putting them through a food mill. Combine the puree with the salt, sugar, melted butter, cream, and Madeira, and whip together well with a spatula or whisk. Spoon the puree into a 1-quart baking dish, dot with butter, and sprinkle with the crumbs or chopped nuts. Bake in a 350° oven for 20 to 30 minutes.

Serving Suggestions: Serve with turkey, pork, or Wild Mushroom Meat Loaf (page 92).

Note: Look out for big-shouldered parsnips. They have a woody core that sometimes needs paring down or cutting out entirely if it's pithy. Parsnips are wonderful keepers, up to 1 month if left unwashed in a perforated bag in the crisper.

Variations:

Form the mixture into small patties, roll lightly in flour, and sauté in 4 to 6 tablespoons butter, turning once, until browned nicely on both sides.

Combine pureed parsnips with an equal amount of pureed potatoes and bake or make into patties and fry.

Cook and puree half carrots and half parsnips. Season the puree with grated fresh ginger and enrich it with a little sour cream. Serve as is or bake as in the recipe.

3 pounds parsnips, cooked
1 teaspoon salt
1 teaspoon sugar
½ to ¾ cup butter (1 to 1½ sticks), melted
3 to 4 tablespoons heavy cream
¼ cup Madeira, or to taste
Additional butter
2 tablespoons bread crumbs or finely chopped nuts for topping

Marian Morash's favorite way with parsnips is simply to slice them very thin and sauté in butter until tender.

Peas and Cucumber in Dill

Sally and Martin Stone

4 tablespoons unsalted butter

2 large cucumbers, pared, cut in half lengthwise, seeded, cut in half again lengthwise, then cut in ½-inch pieces

Salt to taste

1 package (10 ounces) frozen tiny peas, thawed

1 tablespoon snipped fresh dill

Freshly ground pepper to taste

Light and refreshing, quick and simple, prepared with ingredients available anywhere—this recipe can easily become a kitchen standby.

SERVES 4

Melt butter in a sauté pan or large skillet over moderately high heat. When foam subsides add cucumbers and sauté, stirring and tossing, until just crisp-tender, not soft, about 2 minutes. Turn heat to simmer, sprinkle with salt, add peas, and cook, stirring, until heated through, about 1 minute.

Add dill and a generous amount of pepper and toss to combine thoroughly. Transfer to a warm serving dish.

Serving Suggestions: Serve with any fish fillet or chicken breasts seasoned under the skin with Chèvre or minced mushrooms (page 72).

Variations:

Add slivered scallions and blanched matchstick carrots.

Fold in ½ cup or more heavy cream after sautéing the seeded cucumber chunks in butter. Boil over high heat until the cream has reduced and thickened. Serve with plain roasted or poached chicken or fish.

Slivered Snow Peas and Toasted Almonds

(Mange-tout aux amandes grillées)

Madeleine Kamman

This accompaniment is a perfect marriage of color and crunch. We like this dish for company dinners—snow peas always seem to add a festive element.

½ *pound snow peas*
2 *tablespoons clarified butter or oil*
Salt
Pepper from the mill
2 *tablespoons slivered toasted almonds or pignoli nuts*

SERVES 6

Remove the ends of the snow peas and cut them crosswise into ¼-inch-wide strips to match the size of the slivered almonds.

Heat the butter or oil, add the snow peas, and quickly stir-fry for 2 minutes or so. Add salt, pepper, and the slivered nuts. Serve promptly.

Serving Suggestions: Serve with Pork Slices with Prunes (page 102) or Orange-spiced Chicken Wings (page 64).

Tips:
Dry the peas well after rinsing so they stay bright green and crisp when sautéed.

Don't use frozen snow peas, which are always disappointing.

Variations:
Sauté slivered mushrooms (wild or cultivated) separately and combine with the snow peas just before serving.

Sauté slivered scallions or matchstick carrots (precooked in the microwave for 1 minute) along with the snow peas.

POTATOES

We think potatoes are the most soul-satisfying of all the members of the vegetable kingdom. They're also blessedly easy to cook; very few complicated recipes can improve on the simple potato dishes. As with all easy preparations, though, they must be cooked attentively.

Baked Potatoes

Classic perfection is achieved by putting a scrupulously scrubbed and dried russet potato in a hot oven for an hour. No foil, no rubbing with oil, no messing around. (It's a fact that an oiled potato bakes somewhat faster, but it has a soft skin—which disqualifies it for us.)

You can cut the cooking time in half by precooking the potatoes in the microwave for ten minutes, then putting them in the hot oven for half an hour. Zapped potatoes suffer a little in texture, but this method overrides that flaw.

However, we agree with James Beard, who preferred the *over*-baked potato. Two hours in a 450° oven will produce a dark-skinned, pitifully wizened potato with a moist and fluffy center and a thick and crunchy double crust. These potatoes have an Addams family–dinner look, so instead of serving them whole, cut them lengthwise into quarters, drizzle melted butter over them, and sprinkle with chives. For a spicy version, season the butter with garlic and cayenne or chili powder.

Scrub and dry one russet potato per person. Pierce the potato in several places so it won't burst. Place in a preheated 375° oven and bake for 1 hour, or until tender when pierced with a fork. Remove from the oven; just before serving, cut an X in the top and pinch. Season to taste with salt and pepper and top with butter or sour cream or one of the following.

Variations:

The classic baked potato takes all manner of toppings. For a change, use well-drained yogurt instead of sour cream, or try Mexican salsa, or a mixture of crisp bacon and Saga or Stilton cheese, or Roasted Garlic (page 151) mixed with butter.

From James McNair: Make a gutsy salad using over-baked potatoes, quartered and placed on a bed of flavorful greens such as arugula, endive, radicchio, or spinach. Dress the salad simply with a vinaigrette of balsamic vinegar and olive oil.

Stuffed Baked Potatoes

Scoop out the hot flesh of baked potatoes and prepare it like mashed potatoes, adding seasonings to complement the entree. A generous amount of minced fresh herbs and Roasted Garlic (page 156) is perfect. Spoon back into the potato shells. Cover the top with grated Monterey Jack, fontina, or Parmesan. Reheat the potatoes in the oven or under the broiler until the cheese melts.

Sweet potatoes take well to stuffing, but their skins don't hold up as well and they just don't look as pretty, so save them for family dinners.

Twice-baked Sweet Potatoes

For double-baked sweet potatoes (which southerners love), scrub and dry some sweet potatoes and bake them at 425° for 45 minutes. Refrigerate them if you want to keep them a few days. Bake them again at 425° until the skin puffs out like a paper bag. The potatoes will be extremely sweet.

Mashed Potatoes

The secret is a potato ricer. This inexpensive old-fashioned device will guarantee you fluffy mashed potatoes. Or you can use an even more old-fashioned tool, the wire potato masher. If you beat the potatoes in a mixer or try to mash them in the food processor, you may overbeat them and end up with something resembling library paste.

Which potato to mash? Use russets for fluffy potatoes, red waxy potatoes for a creamy, rich flavor.

Peel the potatoes, cut them into equal pieces, and let them sit, covered with cold water, until you're ready to cook them. Rinse the potatoes and change the water at least once. Either boil the potatoes over moderate heat until just tender when pierced or cook them in the microwave. Force the hot potatoes through a potato ricer into a heated bowl containing butter, heavy cream, and salt and pepper. For 1 pound of potatoes you'll need about 4 tablespoons butter and 4 tablespoons heavy cream. Whip and fluff the potatoes with a wooden paddle spoon and taste to adjust the additions. The potatoes are ready when you have to gently nudge a big cloud of them off the spoon.

Variations:

Add minced fresh herbs and/or Roasted Garlic (page 151) soon after you have started beating them.

Use well-drained yogurt instead of cream, particularly if you want to add minced herbs and roasted garlic.

Combine mashed potatoes with other root vegetable purees, such as parsnip, carrot, celery root, or turnip.

Beat an egg yolk or two into cooled mashed potatoes. Season the mixture with minced chives, scallions, or herbs (try mint). Form into little cakes or one large round cake (called a *galette*). Dust the small cakes lightly with flour and sauté them in butter. Swirl the top of the galette with a spatula as though icing a cake, sprinkle with hot Hungarian paprika, and brush with a glaze of beaten egg yolk and cream. Bake in a 325° oven for about 20 minutes, or until golden. Sprinkle with crumbled Roquefort just before serving.

Mashed Sweet Potatoes

Use the same technique as for white potatoes (above). Or simply slightly underbake sweet potatoes, pull off the skin, and break them up into a baking dish; mix with a little melted butter and finish in the oven before serving. Season mashed sweet potatoes with grated fresh ginger, cayenne, and snipped fresh chives. They also blend well with lime zest and coconut cream (instead of heavy cream) or orange zest and a spoonful of orange or tangerine juice concentrate.

Roasted Potatoes

If you're lucky, you had a grandmother who could make these wonderful potatoes without batting an eye, the ones that are crusted with glossy amber crunch and have a soft buttery interior.

The roasted potato needs oil, clarified butter, or, best of all, the drippings from roasting meat to baste it. The most heavenly roasted potato nestles up under the standing rib roast, being bathed continuously by the unctuous drippings of the meat. This technique works just as well for lamb or pork roasts. Unless you're planning to serve lots of pan gravy, baking potatoes are too dry for roasting. A round waxy potato (such as Red Bliss) is the one for this job.

Peel the potatoes and quarter them if they seem especially large. Drop them into boiling water and parboil gently until they just resist the pressure of a sharp knife, about 10 minutes. (Or cook them in the microwave, about 3 to 4 minutes on high for ½ pound of potatoes.) Roll them around in the pan drippings, if you have them, or coat with melted butter or oil. Salt and pepper them and roast at 375° for under an hour, or until they are as brown and crusty as you like them.

Variations:

We have a colleague who gets similar results by soaking raw potatoes in ice water for an hour. This removes the starchy surface and produces a crispy crust. Our parboiling method produces a softer interior.

Season the basting oil with garlic and fresh or dried herbs such as rosemary, thyme, or oregano. Experiment with other seasonings such as chili powder, Cajun herb blends, tandoori spices or jerk seasonings from the Caribbean.

Use a preseasoned oil like hot chili oil for a less traditional result.

Consider the "Swedish fan" cut. Resting the peeled potato in a shallow wooden spoon, cut it into ½-inch crosswise slices, using the sides of the spoon to prevent cutting all the way through. The thinner the slices and the deeper the cut, the more the potato will spread while roasting. Be certain to drizzle the oil down into the cuts so that each segment becomes crispy.

From Joyce Goldstein: Roast several varieties of unpeeled potatoes together now that there are so many appealing new ones available—purple, yellow, Finnish. When roasting baby new potatoes, 30 to 45 minutes should be enough to produce a tender result, since you aren't striving for a crusty rich exterior.

From Paula Wolfert: Use this ancient French method. Arrange 1½ pounds little new potatoes on top of 1½ cups sea salt in an enameled cast-iron casserole. Cover and bake in a preheated 450° oven for 45 minutes to 1 hour. Serve with Roasted Garlic (page 151) kneaded with butter. In effect, the potatoes cook in the steam of sea water, which preserves their flavor and keeps them moist. Save the salt and reuse it.

Oven-fried Sweet Potatoes

Preheat the oven to 450°. Peel and cube (½ inch) one sweet potato per person. Parboil the cubes in boiling salted water for 3 minutes (or zap in the microwave). Drain well and put the cubes in a large bowl. Drizzle enough light olive oil over them to coat all sides (about 1 tablespoon per potato). Carefully toss them to coat the cubes. Arrange in a single layer on a baking sheet and put into the hot oven. Turn the potatoes from time to time. They'll be done in about 30 minutes. Salt and pepper them and serve immediately. The outsides will be crispy and caramelized, the centers unctuously soft.

Sautéed Potatoes

For this you need a potato that will hold its shape in a hot pan and survive a lot of tossing and turning. A waxy potato, not a baking potato, will work best.

Peel the potatoes, since the peels would otherwise slide off in the sautéing process, and parboil them until they are not quite cooked through; drain and set aside to cool. As soon as you can handle them, cut them into cubes, quarters, or thick slices. Be sure they're very dry.

Choose a large skillet and add half oil and half butter or bacon fat, just enough to coat the potatoes well. If they start to stick, add more oil or fat, a little at a time. Cook the potatoes over medium-high heat until they're crisp and golden.

Variations:

Season the oil well over low heat with split and smashed cloves of garlic; remove them before tossing in the potatoes. When the potatoes are done, sprinkle with freshly grated Parmesan.

Mince and sauté onions separately if you like the taste of onion in sautéed potatoes; add them just before serving.

Add fresh herbs or a sprinkling of cayenne pepper.

Sauté the potatoes in as little oil and butter as you can. Remove them from the pan when just lightly golden. Add more butter to the pan and a little curry powder. Cook the curry mixture over low heat to release the flavors. Put the potatoes back in and toss and cook until the curry butter is absorbed. Add some thawed frozen petite peas to these potatoes. This makes a nice accompaniment to sautéed shrimp.

When you're grilling outdoors, think ahead and make Double Bliss Potatoes. They are delicious with any entree.

Steam, parboil, or microwave Red Bliss potatoes, whole or cut in half, until just tender. Roll in vegetable oil and season with salt and pepper. Roast in a grill basket over the coals until nicely charred but not dried out. (Cook extra potatoes on the remaining white coals after you've cooked any entree. They store well and reheat beautifully in the microwave.)

Variation: Cut up leftovers for potato salad, add minced sweet onions, and dress with a generous slathering of homemade mayonnaise with a lot of fresh horseradish grated into it.

Double Bliss Potatoes

This recipe is so extraordinarily good and so versatile that we stole it—from our Washington friend and colleague Carol Mason. It's a welcome change from the usual sticky sweet potato side dishes. You can assemble the gratin long before you bake it, or bake it long before you reheat it, so it's the perfect holiday or party side dish.

Savory Sweet Potatoes with Shiitakes

SERVES 10

Have ready an oiled 2-inch deep gratin dish (10- to 12-cup capacity).

Heat 2 to 3 tablespoons of oil in a sauté pan over medium-high heat and briefly cook 1 pound of stemmed and sliced shiitake mushrooms, just enough to soften them.

Peel and thinly slice 3 pounds of sweet potatoes. Cut a stick of butter into chunks. Grate ½ cup of Parmesan cheese. Layer ⅓ of the sweet potatoes in the gratin dish, dot with ⅓ of the butter, and add salt and pepper to taste. Sprinkle half the Parmesan on top. Toss half the mushrooms over the first layer and repeat the process, ending with a thin layer of potatoes and the rest of the Parmesan. Dot with remaining butter.

Bake covered with foil at 350° for 40 minutes. Remove foil and bake another 20 minutes, until golden brown.

Potato Gratin

Martha Rose Shulman

2 large garlic cloves, cut in half
    lengthwise
3 pounds (9 medium) russet or new
    potatoes, unpeeled (or peeled,
    according to your taste), scrubbed,
    and very thinly sliced
3⅓ cups skim milk
2 large eggs, lightly beaten
About 1 teaspoon salt, to taste
Freshly ground pepper
6 tablespoons freshly grated Parmesan

Here's a low-fat version of one of the richest and most luscious potato dishes ever devised, gratin dauphinois. *Ms. Shulman uses skim milk instead of whole milk or cream, and no butter at all.*

SERVES 6 TO 8

Preheat the oven to 400°. Rub the inside of a large (about 14 × 9 × 2 inches) oval gratin dish all over with the cut side of the garlic.

Slice the remaining garlic into thin slivers and toss with the potatoes. Layer the potatoes and garlic in an even layer in the gratin dish.

Mix together the milk, eggs, and salt and pour over the potatoes. Add a generous amount of pepper.

Place in the preheated oven and bake for about 1 hour to 1 hour and 15 minutes. Every 15 minutes or so, remove the casserole from the oven and, using a knife or a wooden spoon, break up the top layer of potatoes that is drying up and getting crusty and fold it into the rest of the potatoes.

When the gratin is golden and the potatoes tender, sprinkle on the Parmesan and return to the heat. Bake another 15 to 20 minutes, until a golden brown crust has formed on the top. Remove from the oven and serve.

Serving Suggestions: Serve with Veal Scallops with Fennel (page 93), Ham Baked in Cola (page 107), grilled pork tenderloin (page 104), or Grilled Flank Steak (page 87).

Note: Madeleine Kamman is often asked if one can substitute milk for cream in the classic gratin. She thinks it's better to eat the dish less often than to compromise its opulence. If, on second thought, you'd like to indulge, just substitute light cream for the skim milk and eliminate the eggs. Dot the top of the dish with slices of butter.

Variation: Add a whiff of freshly grated nutmeg.

Baked Peppers, Potatoes, and Onions

Marian Morash

Baked mixed vegetables are a spontaneous, almost mindless dish. The vegetables can be cut up and strewn in the pan in the morning. Then let them bake while you soak in the tub before dinner. Marian Morash recommends a heavy green olive oil for this dish.

SERVES 4

1 to 1½ pounds green and red
    peppers
1 pound potatoes
1 large sweet onion
¼ cup olive oil
Salt and freshly ground pepper

*W*ash and clean the peppers and cut into 1½- to 2-inch pieces. Peel the potatoes if thick-skinned; I prefer to use unpeeled new potatoes. Cut the potatoes into 1-inch slices or chunks. Peel the onion and cut into chunks. Place everything in a shallow ovenproof dish and pour over the oil. Rub the vegetables with the oil. Sprinkle with salt and lots of pepper. Bake in a preheated 425° oven for approximately 30 minutes, or until the potatoes are tender.

Serving Suggestions: The roasted vegetables can be a meal in themselves. Without a meat addition, they become lovely vegetarian meals. Almost any combination makes a handsome presentation platter alongside a juicy roast.

Variations:

Morash sometimes adds sausages that have been slightly precooked in the microwave or blanched in water.

Add chicken pieces rubbed with garlic and oil.

Add sprigs of fresh rosemary or thyme and a few unpeeled garlic cloves.

Try different combinations, choosing your favorites from among carrots, parsnips, celery, onions, potatoes, turnips, winter squash, celery root, and yams.

Any of the vegetable and potato combinations can be transformed into a well-balanced light supper by melting fontina, Monterey Jack, or mozzarella over the top.

Herbed New Potatoes with Vermouth

Diane Rossen Worthington

This dish is a particularly pretty, dressed-up version of steamed potatoes with just the right counterpoint of seasoning.

SERVES 4

1½ pounds small new potatoes
2 tablespoons unsalted butter
2 tablespoons dry vermouth
2 teaspoons finely chopped chives
1 tablespoon finely chopped mint
¼ teaspoon salt
⅛ teaspoon white pepper

Scrub the potatoes and peel, if desired, or just peel a ring around the center for a more decorative look. Put in the top of a steamer over boiling water. Cover and steam until tender, 15 to 20 minutes.

Heat the remaining ingredients in a small saucepan over medium heat until the butter is melted. Taste for seasoning.

Transfer the potatoes to a serving bowl and pour the vermouth herb butter over. Serve immediately.

Serving Suggestions: Serve with Salmon Slices with Walnut or Hazelnut Vinaigrette (page 56) or Grilled Swordfish with Mustard (page 58).

Just when you think you've heard of every conceivable way to prepare potatoes, yet another unusual and delicious recipe surfaces. This one is from the ancient city of Matera in Sicily.

Hot Devil Potatoes

(Patate al diavolicchio)

Carlo Middione

2 pounds firm, young, white waxy
   potatoes
Salt
1/3 cup virgin olive oil
3 to 5 teaspoons red pepper flakes, or
   to taste

SERVES 6 OR MORE

*W*ash the potatoes and then place them, unpeeled, in a large pan of cold water to cover. Bring the water to a boil over high heat. When it just begins to boil, lower the heat and maintain a gentle boil for 25 minutes, or until the potatoes are done. They are done when a fork can penetrate easily, but the potatoes must not be too soft or they will fall apart. Remove them from the hot water with a slotted spoon and cool them until you can handle them. Peel them and cut them into 1/4-inch slices. Arrange half of the sliced potatoes in a serving dish that eventually will hold them all and sprinkle with salt. Reserve the other half until later.

Heat the olive oil in a frying pan over high heat. When the oil is hot, add the red pepper flakes. Stir the flakes well and do not let them burn. The oil should be tinged with red. Spoon half of the oil and red pepper mixture over the potatoes in the serving dish. Quickly put the other layer of potatoes over the first layer, add more salt, and then pour the rest of the olive oil and red pepper mixture over them, using a rubber spatula to get it all out of the frying pan. Serve the potatoes immediately or leave them for eating later. Do not refrigerate them.

Serving Suggestions: Serve with Rack of Lamb with Anise and Sweet Garlic (page 116) or Grilled Beef Tenderloin with Roquefort and Red Pepper Butter (page 84).

Potato Cakes
(Tortitas de papa)

Diana Kennedy

Safflower oil for frying
½ pound potatoes, cooked and
    skinned
2 heaped tablespoons finely grated
    queso añejo *or* romano
3 tablespoons finely chopped flat-leaf
    parsley
Sea salt to taste
1 large egg, lightly beaten
Salsa

Here's a great opportunity to make lumpy mashed potatoes without apology. Unlike the gringo potato cakes we're used to, these are more like a croquette.

MAKES 10 TO 12 SMALL CAKES

Heat the oven to 350°. Line a baking sheet with 2 layers of paper toweling, with extra paper on the side for the first frying. Heat oil to about a ½-inch depth in a heavy frying pan.

Crush the potatoes roughly with your hands and work in the rest of the ingredients. Take 1 rounded tablespoon of the mixture and fry the roughly formed cake in the hot oil, turning over from time to time until it is a deep golden color. Drain on the paper toweling. When all the cakes have been fried, transfer them to the baking sheet and reheat until sizzling and a lot more of the oil has exuded—about 10 to 15 minutes.

Serve each cake topped with 1 tablespoon of salsa.

Serving Suggestions: Serve with Orange-spiced Chicken Wings (page 64) or Spicy Skirt Steak with Cinnamon (page 89).

Note: There are some excellent bottled Mexican-style salsas on the market now. We are never disappointed with Jardine's.

Red Radishes Sautéed with Vinegar
(Radis roses sautés au vinaigre)

Madeleine Kamman

Cooked radishes are quite delicious, not to mention unusual. Ms. Kamman says the vinegar isn't essential if you don't like it, but, she points out, without it the radishes will completely discolor.

SERVES 6

Clean the radishes of all black traces and slice them into ⅛-inch slices.

Heat the butter or oil in a frying pan or skillet. Add the radishes, toss well in the butter, and add the vinegar, salt, and pepper. Continue stir-frying until the radishes turn orangy red and become somewhat translucent. Add parsley or chives or a mixture of both.

2 bunches of red radishes
1½ tablespoons clarified butter or oil
1 tablespoon sherry vinegar or other
    vinegar
Salt
Pepper from the mill
Chopped parsley and/or chives

Serving Suggestions: Sautéed radishes are very good with all white meats, especially chicken and turkey breast. This dish has a nice cleansing quality that would make it a good accompaniment for the Thanksgiving turkey.

Skillet Scallions

Edna Lewis

4 bunches scallions
3 tablespoons butter

You've probably never eaten cooked scallions as a side dish before—we hadn't—but they're utterly delicious prepared in this simple way.

SERVES 5

Prepare the scallions by picking off any yellow stems. Cut away the fibrous roots from the bottom. Wash in cold water under tap, then cut the tops down to fit the skillet. Heat the skillet and add the butter. When the foaming stage is reached, put in the scallions. The few drops of water left on the scallions from washing are enough for steaming. Cover the skillet and cook over a moderate fire. Turn them over after about 3 minutes. Total cooking time is about 4 to 5 minutes. Be careful not to overcook; the white part should be a bit crisp, the tops tender, shiny, and green. No salt or pepper will be needed.

Serving Suggestions: Serve with Grilled Swordfish with Mustard (page 58) or Chicken Broiled with Mustard, Herbs, and Bread Crumbs (page 63).

Variations:
Garnish the scallions with a few thawed frozen petite peas. For an elegant version, puree the peas with a dash

of cream and run a ribbon of the puree over the center of the scallion bundle.

Sprinkle the finished scallions with crumbled crisp bacon bits.

Add some minced fresh ginger to the butter.

This is an elegant, delicious, and surprising addition to a company meal. You may do a double-take when you see that the pears are in syrup; in fact, the sweetness has a marvelous chemistry with the spinach.

Spinach and Pear Puree
(La Mousseline d'épinards aux poires)

Roger Vergé

2½ pounds fresh spinach or 3 packages (10 ounces each) frozen spinach
Coarse salt
½ pound whole Bartlett pears in syrup or 1 can (7 ounces) pear halves in syrup
7 tablespoons unsalted butter
Salt
Pinch of freshly grated nutmeg

SERVES 6

*I*f you're using fresh spinach, remove the stems and wash the spinach leaves in several changes of cold water; drain.

In a large saucepan, bring 3 quarts of water and 2 tablespoons of coarse salt to a boil. Add the spinach and let the water return to a boil. Immediately turn the spinach into a colander and drain. Fill the saucepan with cold water and plunge the spinach into it to refresh the leaves; drain again. Squeeze handfuls of the spinach between the palms of your hands to extract all the excess water and form the spinach into compact balls. All this can be done several hours ahead and the spinach refrigerated like this until you prepare the puree.

If you're using frozen spinach, simply thaw it before preparing the puree.

Drain the pears and, if they are whole, remove the stems and cores.

Shortly before serving, place the spinach and pears in a food processor or a food mill and reduce to a fine puree. Melt the butter in a large skillet. When the foam subsides and the butter is a light, nut brown color, add the spinach and pear puree. Season with salt and a pinch of freshly grated nutmeg and stir with a wooden spoon until heated through.

Serve in a warmed vegetable dish.

Serving Suggestions: Serve with Church-Supper Ham Loaf (page 110) or Moghul Roasted Leg of Lamb (page 114).

Note: If you can find hydroponically raised fresh spinach, as we sometimes do in our local supermarket, you won't have to wash it. The flavor will be superior, and it will take even less time to prepare than frozen spinach.

Slow-baked Tomatoes

Martha Rose Shulman after Lulu Peyraud

This intriguing recipe pops up all over Europe—Ms. Shulman learned it from Lulu Peyraud of the Domaine Tempier winery in France. By the end of the long, slow baking time, the tomatoes are intensely sweet, savory, and almost caramelized. These are best served at room temperature.

SERVES 4 TO 6

4 to 6 large ripe fresh tomatoes, cut in
    half horizontally
4 to 6 teaspoons olive oil
Salt and freshly ground pepper
2 to 3 garlic cloves (to taste), minced
    or put through a press
3 tablespoons chopped fresh basil or
    parsley

$\mathcal{P}$reheat the oven to 325°. Place the tomatoes on a baking sheet, cut sides up. Drizzle on the olive oil and sprinkle with salt and pepper to taste.

Bake in the preheated oven for 2 to 3 hours, until the tomatoes collapse and begin to caramelize. Sprinkle with the garlic about halfway through the baking, or at the end, and sprinkle with the herbs just before serving. Serve hot or at room temperature.

Serving Suggestions: Serve with Grilled Beef Tenderloin with Roquefort and Red Pepper Butter (page 84), Rack of Lamb with Anise and Sweet Garlic (page 116), or Baked Cod with Onions and Mint (page 60).

Tip: Store the baked tomatoes in the refrigerator in screw-top jars and use them for topping pasta or pizza, saucing fish, steaks, or chops, or just spooning onto a grilled cheese sandwich.

Variations:

Top with crumbled goat cheese or feta or a dollop of well-drained yogurt, sour cream, or crème fraîche.

From Jo Bettoja: Prepare a tomato sauce with oregano and basil from baked tomatoes. Sprinkle ½ cup grated

Parmesan on top of the tomatoes, cover tightly with foil, and bake at 350° for 30 minutes. Remove the foil and bake another 30 minutes. *Ecco!* The pasta sauce is ready.

EDITORS' KITCHEN

Sautéed Cherry Tomatoes

More often than not, the cherry tomato has better color and flavor than the pitiful hothouse varieties we are subjected to most of the year. When you can buy them at your local farm stand, they're even brighter and sweeter. Lately we've even begun to see tiny yellow pear tomatoes in our supermarket. When you need a colorful and tasty cooked garnish on the plate, try the speediest sauté of all, using all red or mixed red and yellow cherry tomatoes.

Wash the cherry tomatoes and pat them dry. Mince a generous quantity of fresh herbs, such as parsley, chives, basil, tarragon, or dill. Heat a little butter and olive oil together in a skillet large enough to hold the tomatoes in a single layer. When the pan is hot, add the tomatoes. Turn the heat up and roll and toss them for only a minute or so. Don't let the skins pop open or the tomatoes will be mushy. As soon as they are just hot, add the herbs and salt and pepper. Serve immediately.

Tip: If the tomatoes start to pop open, mash them up a bit and turn them into a fresh tomato sauce.

Variation: Splash the tomatoes with balsamic vinegar and sprinkle with parsley.

A lot of people turn up their noses at turnips, but when they're cooked properly they can be sensationally good. Chances are no one will be able to guess what this delectable vegetable is. Only the cook will know.

Turnips à la Comtesse

Eugene Walter

SERVES 3 TO 4

*P*eel the turnips just before you're ready to cook them so they won't discolor. Dice them rather small, then cook in water to cover over medium heat with the sugar, salt, bay leaf, and clove. When they're just pierceable but not mushy (about 5 minutes), drain them well. Remove the clove. Butter lavishly or to your taste, add a glop of cream, a miserly dusting of cloves, and salt and pepper. Hurry the dish to the table.

Serving Suggestions: These turnips go beautifully with ham, especially the Ham Baked in Cola (page 107), and roast pork (pages 97–101).

Note: Buy young turnips; the elderly ones tend to be tough and strong tasting. Young turnips can be wonderfully sweet, delicious eaten raw or shaved into salads.

4 turnips
Pinch of sugar
Pinch of salt
1 bay leaf
1 clove
Unsalted butter
Heavy cream
Ground cloves
Salt
Freshly ground black pepper

Stir-fried Zucchini with Sesame Seeds

(Hobak namul)

Madhur Jaffrey

2 pounds medium zucchini
2 teaspoons salt
4 garlic cloves
1 scallion
3 tablespoons vegetable oil
1 tablespoon sesame oil
2½ tablespoons roasted sesame seeds

This aromatic Korean version of sautéed zucchini is a welcome change from the usual Provençal-style recipes. It has the added virtue of flexibility—you can serve it hot, cold, or at room temperature.

SERVES 6

Trim the zucchini and cut them in half lengthwise. Then cut the halves crosswise into ¼-inch-thick slices and put the slices into a large bowl. Sprinkle 1½ teaspoons of the salt over them, mix well, and set aside for 30 to 40 minutes. Drain thoroughly and pat dry. Meanwhile, peel the garlic and chop it fine. Cut the scallion into very fine rounds along its entire length.

Set a wok over a high heat. When it is hot, put in the vegetable oil. When the oil has heated, put in the garlic. Stir once or twice or until the garlic begins to color. Add the zucchini. Stir and fry for 4 to 5 minutes, or until the zucchini are just done. Put in the remaining ½ teaspoon salt, the scallion, and sesame oil. Stir once or twice. Add the roasted sesame seeds. Stir once and serve. This dish may also be served cold as a salad.

Serving Suggestions: Serve with grilled or roast lamb, salmon, or swordfish. Or use it to dress up the humble hamburger.

Tip: Always salt and drain zucchini before frying, as Ms. Jaffrey suggests; releasing some of the juice before stir-frying or sautéing makes the zucchini taste "meatier" and allows the flavored oil to coat the surface more evenly.

Mix 4 tablespoons light soy sauce and 1 tablespoon wine vinegar along with a pinch of sugar; and add to the cooked zucchini. Drain off any excess liquid, and if you are partial to spicy food, season to taste with hot Chinese chili paste with garlic. Serve at room temperature.

This hearty accompaniment could also stand alone as a light main dish.

Zucchini Stuffed with Corn and Cheese

Marian Morash

SERVES 4

Blanch squash in boiling salted water for 5 minutes. Place under cold water and drain. Halve and scoop out the seeds, forming cavities. Coarsely puree the corn and ricotta cheese in a food processor or food mill. Add the chives (if you wish) and season with salt and pepper. Fill squash halves with the mixture, mounding slightly. Cover with grated Cheddar. Place in a buttered casserole and bake, covered, in a preheated 350° oven for 15 minutes. Uncover and bake 20 to 25 minutes or longer, until the squash is tender and the topping is browned.

2 narrow 6- to 7-inch-long zucchini or yellow squash
1 cup corn kernels
½ to ⅔ cup ricotta
1 to 2 tablespoons snipped chives (optional)
Salt and freshly ground black pepper
¾ cup grated Cheddar

Serving Suggestions: Serve with roasted or grilled chicken or Cornish hen or Spicy Skirt Steak with Cinnamon (page 89).

Variations:

Use yellow summer squash instead of green if you prefer and if your menu allows that pastel visual effect.

Fold the corn kernels in instead of pureeing them with the ricotta, particularly if you use tender white shoepeg corn, which is now available frozen.

Substitute slivers of jarred roasted red peppers with roasted garlic and minced fresh herbs, or a spoonful of your favorite bottled Mexican salsa, or well-drained and shredded canned Italian plum tomatoes, for the corn.

Use grated Parmesan or Monterey Jack, to suit the filling and the character of the entree, instead of Cheddar.

Ten-minute Black Beans with Tomatoes and Coriander

Sally and Martin Stone

American black beans, sometimes called turtle beans, are not only distinctively flavored but capable of taking on numerous culinary guises. The black bean seems to suffer less than others from the commercial canning process, particularly when combined with other vegetables and seasonings.

SERVES 4

*H*eat the oil in a small skillet or saucepan over moderately high heat and add the onion and garlic. Sauté, stirring, until onion is almost translucent but still firm, about 2 minutes. Add tomatoes and cook, stirring frequently, for 2 minutes more.

Add the black beans, Tabasco, and salt and stir to combine. Cover skillet and cook until beans are heated through, about 2 minutes.

Remove from heat and stir in 1 tablespoon of the cilantro. Transfer to serving dish and sprinkle with remaining cilantro. Serve immediately.

Serving Suggestions: Serve with Spicy Skirt Steak with Cinnamon (page 89) or grilled pork tenderloin (page 104).

Note: Look for canned black beans in Latin-American markets or choose a Spanish name brand at the supermarket. The Goya brand is reliable.

1½ tablespoons peanut, corn, or safflower oil

1 medium onion, chopped

1 teaspoon chopped garlic

6 fresh plum tomatoes, peeled, seeded, and chopped or 1 can (14 ounces) Italian plum tomatoes, drained and chopped

1 can (16 ounces) black beans, drained and rinsed

½ teaspoon Tabasco

½ teaspoon salt or to taste

2 tablespoons chopped cilantro

Increase the amount of beans to 2 cans. Add a fat pinch of dried thyme to the sautéed onions and garlic. Or add slivers of leftover baked ham or crisp bits of bacon. Omit the tomatoes and the cilantro. Serve the beans with a dollop of sour cream flecked with cayenne.

Sauté a finely chopped red or green pepper (or better yet, both) with the onion and garlic. Instead of tomatoes, use a small package of frozen corn, thawed under very hot running water and well drained. Toss with oil and vinegar and serve at room temperature.

Lentil Puree

James Beard

Dipping into the baker's spice rack to season lentils produces a remarkably good accompaniment for duck, game, chicken, or pork.

SERVES 6

3 cups lentils
1 tablespoon salt
1 onion stuck with 2 cloves
1 bay leaf
8 tablespoons (1 stick) butter
¼ teaspoon mace
¼ teaspoon ginger
½ cup heavy cream

Cover the lentils with water and add the salt, onion, and bay leaf. Bring to a boil and simmer till the lentils are just tender. Drain, then puree them in a food mill. Melt the butter, add the spices and cream, and beat into the puree. Taste for salt and the balance of spices, and correct as needed. Serve very hot.

Serving Suggestions: Serve with Roast Pork with Bay Leaves (page 97), roast Cornish hen (page 77), or Ham Steaks (page 108).

Tip: Use the food processor instead of the food mill, which gives a perfect texture to this puree; the processor is speedier and gives almost as good a result.

EDITORS' KITCHEN

Along with salt and pepper, white rice is the longest-keeping staple in the kitchen. This means that you can stock up on unusual rices, like southern popcorn rice or Carolina Gold, whenever you see them. And of course it also means that rice is the perfect foundation for impromptu dinners. (Brown rice, however, does not keep well.)

Here are our tried and true, quick and simple, long-grain rice recipes. If you choose specialty rice, follow the instructions on the package. Imported rice will need to be picked over for debris and washed until the water runs clear. Basmati rice takes 1½ cups of water to a cup of rice and cooks in only ten minutes, so be careful not to overcook it. A cup of rice will serve 4 people.

Steamed Rice

Combine 1 cup long-grain rice with 2 cups water, season with salt, and bring to a boil. Lower the heat to a simmer, cover the pot, and cook for 17 minutes, or until all liquid is absorbed and there are little craters in the rice. Turn off the heat and let the rice sit with the lid on the pot for 5 minutes before forking it fluffy.

Pilaf

Heat 3 tablespoons butter or olive oil over medium heat in a skillet with a lid. Add 1 cup rice and stir constantly until the rice turns opaque, about 3 minutes. Pour 2 cups boiling water over the rice and add 1 teaspoon salt. Bring the rice back to a boil while continuing to stir. Cover the pan and turn the heat as low as possible. Be sure the lid is tight. Cook the rice for 17 minutes without lifting the lid. All the liquid should be absorbed. Let stand, covered, for 5 minutes off the heat. Fork the rice fluffy.

Variations:
Add ¼ cup or more chopped onion to the butter or oil and sauté it for a few minutes before adding the rice.

Use homemade or canned chicken or beef broth instead of water.

For Green Rice: Process 1 cup parsley leaves (or ½ cup parsley leaves and ½ cup cilantro leaves) with 1 garlic clove and 1 cup of the stock in the food processor until you have a bright green liquid. Add this with the rest of the stock when you cook the rice. Heat turns the herbs dark, so if you want a bright green color, fold the herbs, with a butter enrichment, into the rice just before serving; the flavor will be less intense.

For Nutty Rice: Add toasted, slivered almonds or pecans or green pistachios and minced fresh dates or currants to the cooked rice.

For Seasoned Rice: Add seasonings, such as curry powder, crumbled saffron threads or powdered saffron, chili powder, and/or cumin, to the butter and cook to release the flavor. For a really fresh taste, add grated lemon zest and minced fresh mint and chives.

For Coconut Rice: Replace the stock with unsweetened canned coconut milk, now available in Asian markets under a Thai label. Don't use canned coconut cream intended for blender cocktails, or you'll end up with dessert.

Fried Rice

One of the best things about cooking rice is the leftovers, which make such tasty mixers for quick suppers. Fried rice is such a favorite of ours that we always double the steamed rice amount so that we'll have plenty left in the refrigerator.

For 2 cups *cold* rice, assemble 2 cups small-dice cooked chicken, duck, ham, or seafood, and vegetables such as broccoli florets, carrot, red pepper, scallions, snow peas, or frozen petite peas. (Cut all vegetables to a similar size so that the rice "carries" the vegetables. Blanch broccoli and carrots to the crisp-tender stage first, so all ingredients cook at the same time.) Warm 3 to 4 tablespoons peanut oil (plus a little hot chili oil, if you like) with minced garlic and ginger in a wok or skillet over high heat. When it's hot, add all the vegetables and meat or seafood. Stir over high heat for about 2 minutes. Crumble the rice, add it, and stir-fry for another 2 to 3 minutes, until the rice crackles. Lower the heat and pour 1 beaten egg around the edges of the rice; it will scramble on the spot. Fold the egg into the rice and add soy sauce to taste or, for "white fried rice," none at all.

Variation: From Bert Greene: Use 3 tablespoons butter, ½ teaspoon red pepper flakes, and ⅓ cup chopped macadamia nuts with 3 cups cooked rice.

Spinach Pilaf

Susan Feniger and Mary Sue Milliken

4 tablespoons unsalted butter
3 bunches spinach, stems trimmed
2 teaspoons salt
1 large onion, diced
1 tablespoon ground cumin
1 teaspoon ground cardamom
1 teaspoon ground coriander
1 teaspoon ground turmeric
2 cups cooked rice, preferably basmati
2 tomatoes, peeled, seeded, and diced

One of the fastest pilafs ever, this is also the most beautiful one we've ever seen. Don't hesitate to stock a couple of unusual spices—you'll make this dish often.

SERVES 4 TO 6

Melt 2 tablespoons butter in a large sauté pan over medium-high heat. Sauté spinach with salt just until leaves are wilted. Reserve.

Melt remaining butter in a medium saucepan over medium-high heat. Sauté onion until lightly browned. Lower heat, add ground spices, and stir briefly. Add cooked rice, tomatoes, and reserved spinach. Cook just enough to heat rice through, stirring well to combine. Serve warm.

Serving Suggestions: Serve with any grilled or sautéed fish fillet or with Moghul Roasted Leg of Lamb (page 114) or grilled veal chops.

Tip: Use canned Italian plum tomatoes if fresh tomatoes are not in season.

Variation: Substitute frozen chopped spinach (two 10-ounce packages), thawed and squeezed dry; the dish will not have so vibrant a color as when made with fresh spinach.

Saffron Risotto

Barbara Kafka

A proper risotto can hardly be made in a hurry, but this microwave version is just about flawless and demands only that you respond to the bell. Since a well-flavored risotto leaves luscious leftovers, we always make the large portion.

SERVES 2

*H*eat butter and oil in a large soup bowl, uncovered, in the microwave oven at 100% for 2 minutes.

Add onion, garlic, and rice; stir to coat. Cook, uncovered, at 100% for 4 minutes.

Add broth, wine, and saffron. Cook, uncovered, for 6 minutes. Stir well and cook for 6 minutes more.

Remove from the microwave. Stir in salt and pepper and serve hot.

Serving Suggestions: Serve with Veal Shanks (page 95) or Sicilian Meatballs with Raisins and Pine Nuts (page 106). Saffron risotto makes an elegant first course for a dinner party, followed by the above entrees.

Tip: To serve 6, increase saffron to 16 threads and multiply all other ingredients by 4. Heat butter in an 11 × 8½ × 2-inch dish or a 10-inch quiche dish. Cook onions for 4 minutes. Add rice and cook for 4 minutes more. Add broth and cook for 9 minutes. Stir and cook for 9 minutes more. Remove from oven and stir in salt and pepper.

Variations:

Mold the cooked risotto in a ring mold, cake pan, or any decorative baking container. Before cooking the risotto, measure the mold to see how many cups of rice you will need to fill it. Line the mold with paper-thin,

1 teaspoon unsalted butter
1 teaspoon olive oil
2 tablespoons minced onion
1 garlic clove, smashed, peeled, and
    minced (optional)
¼ cup arborio rice
1 cup chicken broth
¼ cup white wine
9 threads saffron
Kosher salt
Freshly ground black pepper

overlapping slices of prosciutto and pour the cool risotto into the mold. Cover and refrigerate. When you're ready, preheat the oven to 400° and bake for 20 minutes, then cover with foil and bake for 10 minutes more, or until it is warmed through. Fill the center with sautéed whole mushrooms and tiny sweet peas.

Form cold risotto into 1-inch-thick cakes, like potato cakes. Dust all over with cornmeal and sauté in butter until golden. Risotto cakes are wonderful plain, but a pillow of mascarpone or crème fraîche on top would be sublime.

EDITORS' KITCHEN

CORN DISHES

Corn is America's favorite grain, and ours too. These corn dishes work for almost every meal, from breakfast to supper.

Hominy

Canned hominy—dried soaked hulled corn—is a great pantry item to have on hand (Goya is a good brand). Just rinse and drain it, and it's ready to heat and serve.

Here are some suggestions:

- From Julia Child: Heat rinsed, drained canned hominy in butter; add salt and pepper to taste and a handful of minced herbs, such as parsley, basil, and chives.

- Southwestern style: Cook a bit of chili powder with the butter; add salt and pepper to taste.

- Sauté garlic and onion in vegetable oil or lard; add 3 cups rinsed and drained hominy (two 16-ounce cans). Mix in 1 cup canned chopped green chilies and 1 or

2 canned or minced fresh jalapeños. Garnish with chopped ripe tomatoes and avocado with a squeeze of lime. Serve warm with shredded Monterey Jack.

GRITS

Grits are just ground dried corn. Most people think of grits as breakfast food, but they also make a fine side dish to serve with pork or shrimp. You can make the dish like a casserole or like a soufflé. Stone-ground whole-grain grits are best to use, then quick-cooking, but never instant grits.

SERVES 4

Cheese Grits

Cook 1 cup grits as directed on the package but with milk instead of water. The longer you cook them (up to 1 hour), the tastier they'll be—just add water as needed. Preheat the oven to 375°. While the grits are still hot, fold in ¾ cup grated Cheddar, 2 pressed garlic cloves, 4 tablespoons butter, and ¼ cup chopped scallions, if you like. Stir until the cheese melts, then add 2 lightly beaten eggs and 1 cup milk. Pour the mixture into a buttered 2-quart casserole and bake for about 1 hour. (For a soufflé-style dish, separate the eggs and stir the yolks into the warm grits mixture. Beat the whites until stiff, then fold them into the cooled mixture. Pour into a soufflé dish and bake.)

POLENTA

Although its Italian name sounds very exotic and it's certainly fashionable, polenta is nothing more than cornmeal mush.

Polenta takes all manner of toppings and seasonings extremely well. You can top it with sautéed wild mushrooms seasoned with garlic and thyme, or with fresh tomato sauce, or with caramelized onions with hot pepper flakes. Or season it with a touch of pesto or a squirt of anchovy paste.

Freshly made soft polenta, so favored in the north of Italy, hasn't found the same popularity in this country as the cooled firm polenta that can be cut into wedges and grilled, sautéed, or baked. The make-ahead, store, and reheat capability of polenta makes it a fine choice for busy cooks. Grilled or sautéed polenta, seasoned or topped, makes a splendid first course for a company dinner or a light supper for family when you add grilled sausage or meatballs. You can also fry it crisp in butter (dust the wedges first in cornmeal if you like) for breakfast and serve it drizzled with hot maple syrup.

Most supermarkets stock precooked or instant polenta. It is not quite the real thing (which requires a minimum of 15 minutes), but it tastes good on its own account. The liquid can be water, beef broth, or milk. For polenta that is to be grilled or sautéed later, we prefer milk for a creamier interior and a crusty surface.

SERVES 4

Firm Polenta

Bring 1 quart milk to a simmer in a heavy saucepan. Pour 1 cup instant polenta in a heavy stream into the simmering milk and whisk constantly over medium heat for 5 minutes. Remove from the heat and spread the polenta into a buttered square or rectangular baking pan to a thickness of ½ inch. Cover and refrigerate for at least 1 hour before cutting into wedges to sauté, grill, or bake. (To bake the wedges, drizzle them with melted butter, dust with grated Parmesan, and bake in a hot oven until golden.)

Spoon Bread

Edna Lewis

The packaged spoon bread now on the market is a snap, but so is making spoon bread from scratch. It's really a kind of cornmeal porridge of American Indian origin, much beloved in the South. The white cornmeal used in this recipe makes a particularly delicate dish.

SERVES 5

1 cup water-ground white cornmeal
½ teaspoon salt
2 teaspoons sugar
⅓ teaspoon baking soda
2 teaspoons Rumford Baking Powder
3 medium eggs, beaten
3 tablespoons butter
2 cups buttermilk

𝒫reheat the oven to 400°. Sift the cornmeal, salt, sugar, soda, and baking powder together into a mixing bowl. Make a well in the center and add the beaten eggs. At this time put the butter in an 8 × 8 × 2-inch baking pan or a 1½-quart soufflé dish and set it in the oven to heat. Stir the eggs into the meal vigorously, then pour in the buttermilk, stirring well again. Remove the hot pan from the oven and tilt it around to butter the entire surface. Pour the excess butter into the meal batter, stir quickly, and pour the batter into the hot baking dish. Bake for 35 minutes in the preheated oven. Serve in the pan right from the oven with loads of fresh butter.

Serving Suggestions: Spoon bread can stand on its own for a quick family supper or accompany roasted or grilled meats or poultry. We like ham or sausage with spoon bread and a green salad on the side.

Note: If you can't find the water-ground cornmeal Edna Lewis recommends, search out stone-ground meal from a good mill. Spoon bread is only as good as the meal you use to make it.

This recipe originally called for Royal Baking Powder; however, it is no longer available. It's worth seeking out the Rumford brand, sold in health food stores; it contains no aluminum and leaves no bitter aftertaste.

COUSCOUS

Couscous—granules of the hard-wheat semolina, grainlike pasta that's the national dish of Algeria, Morocco, and Tunisia—is one of our favorites. Preparing and steaming the grain in the traditional way is an elaborate procedure. Thanks to the often dubious miracle of food processing, we can now enjoy this alternative to rice or pasta on a whim. Though it's a far cry from the real thing, precooked or instant couscous is readily available and tastes quite good.

No matter how it's cooked, couscous should be fluffy and tender with the grains separate. If it sticks together like risotto, too much liquid was used and/or it was overcooked. We suggest ignoring the instructions on the box. Try this simple method.

Basic Couscous

A 10-OUNCE BOX SERVES 8

Measure equal volumes of couscous and liquid (water or stock). Pour the liquid over the couscous and let sit for 15 minutes, stirring from time to time. Add flavorings and heat in the microwave or cover with foil and bake in a moderate oven for 20 minutes.

Serving Suggestions: Serve with Moghul Roasted Leg of Lamb (page 114), or Rack of Lamb with Anise and Sweet Garlic (page 116), or Orange-spiced Chicken Wings (page 64). Or serve the vegetable or chick-pea couscous with cooked chicken or lamb on top and pass a bowl of harissa (North African hot-pepper sauce, available in gourmet food stores and some supermarkets), for a mock classic couscous. Or stuff a Cornish hen (page 77) with a cayenne-spiked garlic and onion couscous with slivered almonds or whole pistachios and some snipped dried apricots or dates.

Tip: Prepare the couscous with chicken stock, which gives it more character; taste canned broth for saltiness and adjust the amount of salt accordingly.

Variations:
Add minced garlic and onion to a little butter and sauté in a saucepan (or zap in the microwave) until soft; proceed with the recipe.

Stove-top Method: Add minced shallot to a little butter in a saucepan. Stir in a big pinch of ground cinnamon, ¼ teaspoon ground cumin, and ¼ cup dried currants along with the broth and a pinch of salt. Add couscous. Bring the mixture to a boil. Then lower the heat and cook gently, covered, for 5 minutes. Garnish with toasted pine nuts.

Add chopped cooked vegetables, such as carrots, zucchini, parsnips, broccoli, tomatoes, onion, and peas, to the finished couscous.

Add rinsed and drained canned chick peas and chopped fresh cilantro to the couscous.

Dress cooled couscous with a lemon and roasted-garlic (page 151) vinaigrette and sprinkle with chopped fresh mint.

Quick Breads

QUICK BREADS

Custard-filled Cornbread

Spiced Masa Muffins

Southern Biscuit Muffins

Cream Biscuits

Popovers

Huffy Puffy

Banana Nut Bread

American Bean Bread

Red Pepper and Cheese Bread

Icelandic Three-grain Brown Bread

Beer Rye Bread

Cheese Crackers

othing, not even potatoes, can equal the joy and comfort of homemade bread. Even for those of us who love to bake, it's increasingly hard to find the time for double risings and long hours in or near the kitchen. So here we offer some unusual quick breads we think are particularly successful. There are also some homemade crackers—a touch guaranteed to earn the admiration of your guests—and some great old standards much in need of revival, such as Southern Biscuit Muffins and Banana Nut Bread. Even if you're only serving soup or a salad with homemade bread for a lunch, the freshly baked bread will make it a special occasion.

Custard-filled Cornbread

Marion Cunningham after Marjorie Kinnan Rawlings

2 eggs
3 tablespoons butter, melted
3 tablespoons sugar
½ teaspoon salt
2 cups milk
1½ tablespoons white vinegar
1 cup all-purpose flour
¾ cup yellow cornmeal
1 teaspoon baking powder
½ teaspoon baking soda
1 cup heavy cream

We're sure you already have your own favorite cornbread recipe, but unless it's this one, with a delectable creamy center, you need one more. The novelist Marjorie Kinnan Rawlings published a much sweeter version in the Thirties in her book Cross Creek Country.

SERVES 8

Preheat the oven to 350°. Butter an 8-inch-square baking dish or pan that is about 2 inches deep. Put the buttered dish or pan in the oven and let it get hot while you mix the batter.

Put the eggs in a mixing bowl and add the melted butter. Beat until the mixture is well blended. Add the sugar, salt, milk, and vinegar and beat well. Sift into a bowl or stir together in a bowl the flour, cornmeal, baking powder, and baking soda and add to the egg mixture. Mix just until the batter is smooth and no lumps appear.

Pour the batter into the heated dish, then pour the cream into the center of the batter—*don't stir.* Bake for 1 hour, or until lightly browned. Serve warm.

Spiced Masa Muffins

Abby Mandel

At the other end of the spectrum from cornbread, these fluffy, light corn muffins have a marvelous, earthy flavor and a sweetly fragrant aroma. Masa harina, the flour that's used to make tortillas, is usually available in Latin American markets.

MAKES 8 MUFFINS

Fifteen minutes before baking, place the rack in the center of the oven and preheat oven to 375°. Line 8 muffin cups with paper liners or grease the cups.

To make in a food processor, process the flour, masa or cornmeal, baking powder, pepper flakes, baking soda, salt, sugar, sour cream, oil, and eggs for 3 seconds. Run a spatula around the sides of the work bowl and process again just until mixed, 1 to 2 seconds.

To make by hand, put the flour, masa or cornmeal, baking powder, pepper flakes, baking soda, salt, and sugar in a mixing bowl and stir to combine. Break up the eggs with a fork and add to the dry ingredients along with the sour cream and oil. Mix just enough to combine.

Divide the batter among 8 muffin cups. Bake until light brown, about 25 minutes. Let muffins cool in the cups for 5 minutes, then turn out onto a rack. Serve warm.

Tip: Unless you want to strike a match on your tongue, we suggest that you reduce the amount of red pepper flakes, especially if you're opening a new and potent jar.

1 cup unbleached all-purpose flour
½ cup masa harina or finely ground yellow cornmeal
2 teaspoons baking powder
1 teaspoon crushed red pepper flakes
½ teaspoon baking soda
½ teaspoon salt
¼ cup sugar
¾ cup sour cream
½ cup safflower oil
2 large eggs

Southern Biscuit Muffins

Craig Claiborne

2¼ cups flour
Salt to taste (optional)
3 tablespoons sugar
1½ teaspoons baking powder
10 tablespoons butter, at room
   temperature
1 cup buttermilk

These buttermilk biscuits are baked in muffin tins—not exactly traditional, but very easy, and Craig Claiborne claims they're the best biscuits he's ever eaten. We had exactly the same reaction.

MAKES 12 BISCUITS

Preheat the oven to 350°.

Sift together the flour, salt, sugar, and baking powder into a mixing bowl.

Cut the butter into small pieces and add it. Using the fingers or a pastry cutter, work the butter into the dry ingredients until it has the texture of coarse cornmeal. Add the buttermilk and stir to blend without overmixing.

Spoon the mixture into a muffin-tin pan with 12 indentations, each with a ⅓-cup capacity. Place in the oven and bake 40 to 45 minutes, until crusty and golden brown on top.

Note: All buttermilk is low-fat, but look for cultured buttermilk or keep a can of dried buttermilk powder in the cupboard to use for baking.

Cream Biscuits

James Beard

These are the famous biscuits of Beard's childhood as made by the family Chinese cook. They're so ridiculously simple to make that you barely need to be awake to bake a batch. Without a doubt, they make the very best strawberry shortcake.

MAKES ABOUT 12 BISCUITS

Sift the dry ingredients together and fold in the heavy cream until it makes a soft dough that can be easily handled. Turn out on a floured board, knead for about 1 minute, and then pat to a thickness of about ½ to ¾ inch. Cut in rounds or squares, dip in melted butter, and arrange on a buttered baking sheet or in a square baking pan. Bake in a preheated 425° oven for 15 to 18 minutes and serve very hot.

2 cups all-purpose flour
1 teaspoon salt
1 tablespoon double-acting baking powder
2 teaspoons granulated sugar
¾ to 1 cup heavy cream
Melted butter

EDITORS' KITCHEN

Popovers are a snap, no matter what you've heard to the contrary. They're also a special treat for company, since most of us don't think to make them for ourselves.

Popovers

MAKES 9 OR 10 POPOVERS

Do not preheat the oven. Butter either nine 6-ounce ovenproof glass custard cups or a 10-cup muffin tin.

Mix 1 cup sifted all-purpose flour with ¼ teaspoon salt; add 1 tablespoon melted butter, 1 cup milk, and 2 large eggs, at room temperature. Process until very smooth or beat with an electric mixer at medium-high speed for 2 to 3 minutes. Fill the prepared cups or tins halfway.

Set the oven at 400° and bake the popovers on the center rack for about 40 minutes for a popover with a dark crust and a fairly moist interior. If you like it drier inside with a paler crust, set the oven at 375° for about 50 minutes. Either way, *never open the oven door until the time is up*—popovers will collapse in a draft.

Tips:
Always start popovers in a cold oven.

Prick the popovers with a toothpick after they're baked and loosen them from the cups or tin if you don't like any moist dough inside; tip them on their sides and put them back in the oven, with the heat off and the door ajar, for about 10 minutes.

Huffy Puffy

The closest thing to a popover, aside from Yorkshire Pudding, is the Swedish Oven Pancake, a.k.a. Huffy Puffy, Dutch Babies, or any number of nicknames. This more eggy version is baked in a shallow pan. The proportions given are per person; you can just about memorize this recipe and produce it on the spot, multiply it as necessary, and add tidbits to taste, sweet or savory.

FOR EACH SERVING

Preheat the oven to 475°.

Put 2 tablespoons butter in a small iron skillet or gratin pan and set it in the oven to melt; watch to see that it doesn't burn. Beat 1 large egg with a whisk, gradually whisk in ¼ cup milk and then ¼ cup flour until the batter is smooth. As soon as the butter is melted, add the batter and return the pan to the oven for about 15 minutes, or until it's risen and golden. The pancake will rise on the sides and collapse in the center.

Variations:

Add minced herbs, such as parsley, chives, or dill, to the batter.

Add grated cheese to the batter.

Add sautéed onion, ham slivers, and apples to the butter before pouring the batter into the pan.

Fill the puff with sugared berries or glazed apple slices.

Fill it with creamed chicken and ham or a well-seasoned fresh mushroom ragout for a light supper or casual company starter.

Banana Nut Bread

Susan Feniger and Mary Sue Milliken

It takes about ten minutes to make this particularly delicious banana nut bread. We always forget how good it is—and how welcome—at the breakfast or brunch table with whipped cream cheese, or as an accompaniment to a luncheon fruit salad. Considering all the dark-skinned Chiquitas we discover at the bottom of the fruit bowl, it's a good thing we like this bread so much. The ripest bananas make the best banana bread.

MAKES 1 LOAF

$\mathcal{P}$reheat the oven to 325°. Butter a 9 × 5 × 3-inch loaf pan.

Cream butter and sugar until light and fluffy. Add eggs, one at a time, beating well after each addition.

In a small bowl, mash bananas with a fork. Mix in milk and nuts.

In another bowl, mix together flour, salt, baking soda, and baking powder.

Add banana mixture to creamed mixture and stir until combined. Add dry ingredients, mixing just until flour disappears.

8 tablespoons (1 stick) butter, softened
1 cup granulated sugar
2 large eggs
3 ripe bananas
1 tablespoon milk
1 cup coarsely chopped walnuts
2 cups all-purpose flour
1 teaspoon salt
1 teaspoon baking soda
1 teaspoon baking powder

Pour batter into pan and bake 1 hour to 1 hour and 10 minutes, until a toothpick inserted in the center comes out clean. Set aside to cool on rack in pan about 15 minutes. Remove from pan, invert, and cool completely on rack.

Tip: Overripe bananas, peeled first, freeze very well, so you can collect them and make this bread when you need it.

Variations:

Substitute unsalted macadamia nuts, pecans, or dry-roasted pistachios for the walnuts. Snipped dried apricots make a nice tart addition.

Substitute dark rum for the milk.

Add a heaping teaspoon of freshly grated ginger to the batter or serve with cream cheese mixed with minced crystallized ginger.

This is a surprisingly good quick bread, with a flavor that's reminiscent of tortillas. Try the bean cakes; they are very good with pork, game, and hearty stews, or with vegetarian meals (with complementary beans and corn, the bread or the bean cakes are a complete protein).

American Bean Bread

Bill Neal

MAKES 1 SMALL LOAF

Combine all the ingredients, beating just enough to make a smooth batter. Turn into a greased 8 × 5 × 2¾-inch loaf pan and bake 45 to 50 minutes in an oven pre-heated to 375°. When top browns and sides pull away from the pan, turn out and cool on a rack. Delicious warm with butter.

Variation: Bill Neal suggests making bean cakes with the bread batter (half the amount is enough for 4 servings). Drop the batter by the large tablespoon into ¼ inch of hot fat, preferably lard. Cook well, turning once, until nicely brown, crisp, and puffed.

1⅔ cups cooked, sieved pinto beans or one 15-ounce can pinto beans with liquid, sieved
1½ cups cornmeal
2 eggs, beaten
¾ cup buttermilk
Salt to taste, about ½ teaspoon
1 teaspoon baking soda

EDITORS' KITCHEN

This very good recipe literally fell into our laps while we were looking through a beloved but long-unused bread cookbook. We have no idea who gave it to us, but the note at the top says: "Good & easy—excellent toast—use half red, half green at Christmas." We tried it again, and all those comments are accurate.

Red Pepper and Cheese Bread

8 tablespoons (1 stick) butter, softened

3 eggs

1 cup self-rising flour

1 cup grated cheese, such as Monterey
   Jack, Cheddar, or Gruyere

½ teaspoon salt

Dash of cayenne pepper

1 red pepper, minced

1 small to medium onion, minced

Preheat the oven to 375°.

Beat together the butter and eggs. Add the rest of the ingredients and blend well. Pour into a buttered 8 × 5 × 2¾-inch loaf pan and bake 50 minutes. Cool and slice.

Tip: Self-rising flour has baking powder and salt already added. To substitute ordinary flour, use the 1 cup measure but replace 1 teaspoon of ordinary flour with 1 teaspoon baking powder and ½ teaspoon salt.

Icelandic Three-grain Brown Bread (Brunbraud)

Beatrice Ojakangas

½ cup brown sugar, packed

½ cup butter, softened

1 cup rolled oats

1 cup dark rye flour

2 cups whole wheat flour

2 cups all-purpose flour

1 teaspoon salt

4 teaspoons baking soda

2½ cups buttermilk

This soda bread recipe comes from an Icelandic farmhouse—it's dark, delicious, and full of wholesome grains. It's also excellent toasted.

Preheat the oven to 350°. Grease two 9 × 5 × 3-inch loaf pans.

In a large bowl, cream together the brown sugar and butter. Mix the rolled oats, rye flour, whole wheat flour, all-purpose flour, salt, and baking soda together in another bowl, then add to the creamed mixture along with the buttermilk. Mix until well blended. Divide the mixture between the two pans and smooth the tops. Bake 1 hour or until a wooden skewer inserted in the center comes out clean. Turn out of pans and cool on racks.

Tip: Mix 2½ cups milk and 2½ tablespoons fresh lemon juice or vinegar to substitute for the buttermilk if you have none.

EDITORS' KITCHEN

There are a couple of good packaged beer-bread mixes on the market now, but few recipes in cookbooks. This is such a simple and delicious bread with very good keeping qualities that we developed our own.

Beer Rye Bread

MAKES 1 LOAF

𝒫reheat the oven to 350°.

Mix the dry ingredients together and stir in the beer until the mixture is sticky. Do not overmix. Spoon the batter into a well-buttered 9 × 5 × 3–inch bread pan and bake for 30 minutes. Slide the pan to the front of the oven rack and pour the melted butter over the top. Bake another 30 minutes or until the loaf sounds hollow when tapped on top. Cool in pan for a few minutes, then turn out on a rack.

2 cups self-rising flour
1 cup rye flour
1 tablespoon sugar
3 tablespoons caraway seeds (optional)
¾ teaspoon baking powder
¼ teaspoon baking soda
1 teaspoon salt
12 ounces golden beer, such as Molson's Golden Ale
3 tablespoons butter, melted

Cheese Crackers

Marilyn M. Moore

½ cup (1 stick) butter

2 cups (8 ounces) grated sharp
    Cheddar

2 cups unbleached all-purpose flour,
    sifted

1 egg yolk mixed with 1 tablespoon
    milk

These rich crackers come to us courtesy of the Hecker's and Ceresota flour folks. Crackers are a snap to make—if you can roll out dough, that's all that's required. These cheese crackers are great with soups or salads. Fresh out of the oven, they're a charming addition to a canapé assortment.

MAKES 42 CRACKERS

Cream together the butter and cheese until light. Gradually blend in the flour. Wrap and chill the dough for 1 hour or longer.

Preheat the oven to 325°. On a lightly floured surface, roll to ¼ inch thickness. Cut into 2-inch squares. Place squares on an ungreased baking sheet. Brush tops of squares with the egg yolk–milk glaze. Bake for 15 to 20 minutes, or until golden brown. Cool on wire racks.

Desserts

DESSERTS

Coeur à la Crème with Raspberry Sauce

Raspberry Sauce

Lemon Curd Mousse

Pots de Crème

Baked Maple Custard

Panettone Bread Pudding

Blueberry Gingerbread

Gingersnap Dessert

Shortbread

Bittersweet Brownies

Soft Almond Paste Cookies

Toasted Hazelnut Cookies

Pinch Pie

Press-in Tart Crust

Pecan Pie Filling

Cookie-crumb Crust

Crumb Crust Cheesecake

Puff Pastry Crust

Almond Base for Fruit Tarts

Lemon Curd Napoleons

Chocolate–Chestnut Log

Chocolate–Amaretti Torte

Chocolate Sauce

Instant Berry Granita

Fresh Lime Ice Cream

Pineapple in Port Wine

Mango Compote

Alice's Cherry Compote with Balsamic
    Vinegar

Fruit Compotes

Antiguan Charcoal-baked Bananas

Dried Apricots Baked with Vanilla

*A*lthough Americans have always had a great fondness for the dessert extravaganza—remember Baked Alaska?—health consciousness is forcing us to hone our palates to more sensible pleasures. Good news for the hurried cook, who can serve beautiful fruit compotes or a selection of little tidbits along with a dessert wine. Often we can satisfy our longing for sweet endings by having something quite small but intense, just one perfect chocolate truffle, for instance.

The most important point about dessert is that it should balance with the rest of the meal. Because your guests will linger over dessert and coffee, it has—like the last word in a sentence—the strongest emphasis. If the meal has been at all rich, the light, clean essences of lemon, lime, orange, pineapple, or mint will give you a staccato finale. So will a strong coffee flavor, particularly since a lot of people no longer drink the real thing.

After a groaning board holiday meal, fresh fruit is very restorative; on the other hand, if you've had a low-fat grilled fish or chicken entree with pristine fresh vegetables or salad, an indulgent dessert like cheesecake is certainly in order. Just be sure there's also something light for those who really don't want to be tempted.

Last-minute company is the biggest challenge of all. One of us had to face that reality recently and had only thinking time to produce dessert. Some monstrous long-stemmed strawberries had fortunately leaped straight into the shopping cart earlier in the day, and a quick run to a French pastry shop produced a gorgeous almond-covered brioche split and filled with rum custard cream. It was quickly surrounded with the strawberries, and into a basket went a stash from the cupboard: the last of the glazed apricots, some chocolate-covered espresso beans, some minted almonds, and a few shards of homemade coconut almond bark. Everyone was happy, from the active dieter (who stuck to the strawberries) to the vegetarian (who liked the apricots and nuts) to the supremely indulgent (who ate it all). And that, we think, is what it's all about.

Coeur à la Crème with Raspberry Sauce

Patrick O'Connell

8 ounces cream cheese, softened
⅔ cup confectioners' sugar
1¼ cups heavy cream
1 teaspoon vanilla extract
1 teaspoon freshly squeezed lemon
   juice
1 teaspoon framboise
Raspberries for garnish
Raspberry Sauce (recipe follows)

This classic dish isn't often served at home, probably because people think it's complicated to make and requires the traditional heart-shaped porcelain mold. In fact, this version, which is served at The Inn at Little Washington in Virginia, is made in moments. If you don't have the right mold, never mind; just use a basket lined with cheesecloth or with a kitchen towel. Remember to make this dessert a day ahead.

SERVES 6

Beat the cream cheese in a mixer and add the confectioners' sugar.

In a separate bowl, beat the cream until it's whipped. Fold the two mixtures together and add the vanilla, lemon juice, and framboise. Line individual heart molds, or one large mold, or a small basket with dampened cheesecloth. Spread the mixture evenly into the mold, cover with plastic wrap, and refrigerate overnight with a drip pan under the mold.

To serve, unmold the cheese and surround with additional raspberries and sauce.

Raspberry Sauce

1 pint raspberries
½ cup superfine sugar
2 teaspoons freshly squeezed lemon
   juice
Framboise to taste

Puree 1 pint fresh raspberries in the food processor with ½ cup superfine sugar, 2 teaspoons fresh lemon juice, and framboise to taste. Strain the seeds through a fine-mesh strainer.

Tip: Substitute low-fat cream cheese (sometimes called neufchatel) for regular cream cheese.

Variation: Make the sauce with strawberries and cassis instead of raspberries and framboise.

Lemon Curd Mousse

Anne Rosenzweig

This is one of the most delicious lemon desserts we've ever eaten. Anne Rosenzweig serves it in her own tissue-thin tuiles, but we are content just to spoon it out of sherbet glasses. Fresh raspberries are a wonderful foil for the richness of the mousse.

SERVES 6 TO 8

2 large eggs
2 egg yolks
½ cup plus 1 tablespoon sugar
7 tablespoons fresh lemon juice, strained
1 tablespoon grated lemon zest
9 tablespoons unsalted butter, chilled
2 cups heavy cream

*W*hisk the whole eggs and yolks together, then add the sugar, lemon juice, and zest.

Place the mixture in a heavy bottomed pan, stir over moderate heat, and add the butter in bits. Continue to stir for about 4 minutes, or until it begins to thicken. Never let the mixture boil. When thick as pudding, remove from heat, pour into a bowl, and cover the surface with plastic wrap, piercing it so that steam escapes but no crust can form. Chill.

When the mixture is thoroughly cold, whip the cream until moderately stiff and fold into the lemon curd.

Serving Suggestions: Heap the mousse into the Pinch Pie meringue (page 234) or the gingerbread crumb crust (page 237). Garnish with fresh mint sprigs or ring the edge with berries.

Serve with Blueberry Gingerbread (page 226) or line a puff pastry crust (page 238) and top with berries.

Buy tuiles or individual meringues at the bakery and fill with the mousse.

Variation: Cut the cream to 1 cup for the best and lemoniest result.

Pots de Crème

Pots de crème are always a wild success, rich as truffles if you use cream, relatively low-fat if you opt for two-percent-fat milk. Either way, this may be the fastest dessert you'll ever make.

SERVES 6

Break up 7 squares (7 ounces) semisweet chocolate—or use chocolate chips—and chop in the food processor. In a small saucepan over medium heat, bring to a boil 1 cup light cream or 2% milk. Add the hot cream or milk and process until smooth. Add 1 egg and 1 tablespoon brandy or rum and process until incorporated. Pour into 6 little cups and refrigerate until serving time, at least 2 hours.

Baked Maple Custard

Ken Haedrich

4 large eggs, lightly beaten
½ cup maple syrup
1 teaspoon vanilla extract
¼ teaspoon salt
3 cups milk, heated just to the boiling
    point

Baked custard may sound pedestrian, but in fact this is a very special custard because of its maple syrup. We've yet to meet the person who doesn't love maple custard, which is particularly soothing served glassy cold on a hot summer's day.

SERVES 6

Preheat the oven to 350°. Bring about 4 cups of water to a boil and reserve.

    With a whisk, gently blend together the eggs, maple syrup, vanilla, and salt. Slowly stir in the hot milk. Ladle into custard cups, filling each to within ¼ inch of the rim. Place the cups in a large, shallow casserole and carefully pour the boiled water into the pan, until it comes about halfway up the cups. Bake for about 50 minutes, until the edges seem set but the middle a bit wiggly; they'll finish cooking as they cool. Serve warm, or cool to room temperature, cover, and chill.

Serving Suggestions: We would never turn down cookies and custard for dessert, but maple custard for breakfast, now that's a real treat. Try it for a company brunch with fresh berries or nestled next to a cinnamon-poached pear.

Tips:

From Edna Lewis: Use a fork to break the egg yolks rather than a whisk, which she says beats too much air into the yolks; if you whisk up a froth on the custard, that foam will set up in the oven and bake your custard into tough layers.

Make the custard in a 2-quart soufflé dish or any deep round pan or glass casserole.

Take the custard from the oven while the very center still jiggles a bit to avoid overbaking, which causes it to weep; the custard will finish cooking after it leaves the oven.

Cook the custard in the microwave: Place 4 filled custard cups in a 1-inch water bath on High for 5 minutes; if not done, check at 1½-minute intervals, taking them out when they're still wet at the center.

Variation: Dust a little freshly grated nutmeg and a spoonful of sugar over the top of the custard just before it goes into the oven.

Panettone Bread Pudding

Alice Waters and Paul Bertholli

4 cups milk
11 tablespoons sugar
5 whole eggs
5 egg yolks
1 teaspoon vanilla extract
⅓ loaf panettone
2 tablespoons unsalted butter

Almost everyone loves bread pudding, and this elegant version should delight them all. Panettone, the airy, lightly sweet Italian holiday bread, comes in a nifty box with a ribbon handle; be extravagant and buy yourself one.

SERVES 12

*H*eat the milk with the sugar until it is just hot and the sugar has dissolved. Place the eggs and egg yolks in a bowl. Whisk in the hot milk until well combined. Stir in the vanilla extract and strain the custard through a fine-mesh sieve into a bowl.

Preheat the oven to 350°.

Slice the panettone into pieces ¼ inch thick and cut each slice in half. Place on a baking sheet and bake for 6 to 8 minutes, or until crisp and lightly toasted. Melt the butter and brush one side of the panettone slices with it. Arrange the slices evenly in a baking dish (8 × 8 inches), pour the custard over the slices, and let stand for 15 minutes. Place the dish of bread pudding in a larger baking dish containing enough hot water to come halfway up the sides of the bread pudding. Bake for about 35 to 40 minutes. When the custard puffs around the sides of the baking dish and is only just set in the center, the pudding is done. Remove from the water bath and cool slightly. Serve while still warm.

Serving Suggestions: This is a perfect brunch dessert or a follow-up to a light salad meal.

Tips:

Add a light dusting of freshly grated nutmeg to the milk.

Get a Christmas panettone and substitute 4½ cups of eggnog for the custard.

Substitute challah if there's no panettone available.

Cook any leftover custard mixture in a bowl in the microwave, set on low, giving the dish a quarter turn every 2 minutes; remove it when it still jiggles a bit.

Note: Panettone usually appears in Italian and gourmet specialty shops in late fall for the holidays. The loaves come in several sizes. Panettone keeps exceedingly well, so you might consider stocking up since it's not always available year-round.

Blueberry Gingerbread

Lisa Yockelson

1½ cups unsifted *cake flour*

1 teaspoon baking powder

¼ teaspoon baking soda

¼ teaspoon salt

2 teaspoons ground ginger

1½ teaspoons ground cinnamon

½ teaspoon freshly grated nutmeg

¼ teaspoon ground allspice

⅔ cup fresh blueberries, picked over

8 tablespoons (1 stick) unsalted butter, softened at room temperature

½ cup plus 3 tablespoons vanilla-scented granulated sugar or plain granulated sugar

5 tablespoons light molasses

1 extra-large egg, at room temperature

2 extra-large egg yolks, at room temperature

½ cup sour cream, at room temperature

Confectioners' sugar for dusting (optional)

Here two New England classics are married in a wonderfully spicy dark gingerbread. This homey cake slices beautifully, so it's a good choice for a picnic or the buffet table.

MAKES ONE 8-INCH ROUND CAKE

Lightly butter and flour an 8-inch round springform pan; set aside. Preheat the oven to 350°.

Sift the flour with the baking powder, baking soda, salt, ginger, cinnamon, nutmeg, and allspice onto a large sheet of waxed paper. Put the blueberries in a bowl and toss with 1 tablespoon of the sifted mixture.

Beat the butter in the large bowl of an electric mixer on moderately high speed for 2 minutes. Beat in the sugar; beat for 2 minutes. Beat in the molasses. Add the egg and beat it in; beat in the egg yolks. With the mixer on low speed, alternately add the sifted dry ingredients in 2 additions and the sour cream in 1 addition, beginning and ending with the dry ingredients. By hand, fold in the floured blueberries. Spoon the batter into the prepared pan. Gently push the batter about ¾ inches up the sides of the baking pan with a small spatula, to help the batter rise evenly as the cake bakes.

Bake the cake on the lower-third-level rack of the preheated oven for about 40 to 45 minutes, or until a wooden pick inserted in the center of the cake comes out without any particles of cake clinging to it. The cake will pull slightly away from the sides of the pan when done.

Let cool in the pan on a wire rack for 10 minutes, then remove the hinged ring of the pan. Let cool completely. (If you are transporting the cake to a picnic, leave the outer band on for traveling.) Dust the top of the cake with a little confectioners' sugar, if you like.

Serve the cake cut in wedges.

Serving Suggestions: Try this with lemon ice cream or a big dollop of unsweetened whipped cream on top.

Variations:

If you're fresh out of vanilla-scented granulated sugar, add 1 teaspoon vanilla extract with plain sugar.

Substitute dried wild blueberries for fresh (never frozen) blueberries.

Make the gingerbread with chopped candied ginger or currants and walnuts instead of blueberries.

Gingersnap Dessert

Diana Kennedy

This dessert comes from an unlikely source: the world's greatest authority on Mexican cuisine. Mrs. Kennedy calls it "a silly dessert" and it is—reminiscent of refrigerator desserts of the Fifties. But this is a very sophisticated version, and inexplicably delicious. The flavor only improves if it's made several days ahead.

SERVES 6

⅔ cup heavy cream
½ cup finely chopped preserved or crystallized ginger, or to taste
24 thin ginger cookies, about 2½ inches in diameter

$\mathcal{W}$hip the cream until stiff and stir in the pieces of ginger. Spread one of the cookies with a thick coating of cream, top with another cookie, and repeat twice again until there are 4 layers of cookies. Decorate on top with a dab of cream and a small piece of ginger.

 Have ready a shallow dish into which the 6 layered cookies can be placed side by side with at least ½ inch between them. Cover the dish with plastic wrap and place in the freezer overnight. Two hours before serving time, remove from the freezer and let the cookies come up to just below room temperature to serve. They are best left for several days in the freezer before eating.

Serving Suggestions: This is not the right finish to a formal dinner, but it's extremely refreshing after an exotic spicy meal.

Tip: Homemade ginger cookies are best, but you can use the Swedish ginger thins now available in most supermarkets if you don't have the homemade.

EDITORS' KITCHEN

Shortbread

This is the dessert we always make if we're caught without any dessert, and it's always a big hit. It's homey, it looks great, and it melts in your mouth. Many shortbread recipes call for instant flour, powdered sugar, rice flour, or cornstarch—all of which produce a more refined texture. We prefer this rustic version, which is also less fussy to prepare.

MAKES ABOUT 26 SHORTBREAD PIECES

Preheat the oven to 325°. Butter an 8-inch pie pan or square pan and set aside.

Put in a mixing bowl 1 scant cup cool butter, cut in chunks, ½ cup light brown sugar, and 2 cups all-purpose flour. Work the butter into the flour and sugar with your fingers until you have a shiny dough ball. Don't overwork it or the shortbread will be hard and compact instead of crispy. Pat the dough into the pan (don't worry if it's rough-looking). Prick the shortbread all over with a fork, making an interesting design. Make a border of tine marks all around the edge. Bake the shortbread for 50 minutes to 1 hour, or until lightly browned. Cool in the pan. When you're ready to serve the shortbread, break it into small pieces with a fork and pile them up on a plate.

Variations:

Add ¼ cup minced candied ginger, a handful of chocolate chips, or 1 teaspoon ground cardamom.

Add dry-roasted peanuts, pecans, or hazelnuts. Toast the pecans or hazelnuts first on a cookie sheet in a 350° oven; they're ready when they start to smell good.

Make the shortbread with whole wheat flour but not whole wheat *pastry* flour, which will make the shortbread a bit too crumbly.

Bittersweet Brownies

Jo Bettoja

Everyone loves brownies, and these are grown-up, sophisticated brownies, intensely chocolate and not too sweet. They're so rich that you should serve just a little square, as though they were candies.

MAKES 32 (2-INCH) OR
64 (1-INCH) BROWNIES

Preheat the oven to 350°. Have ready a greased 8- or 9-inch square baking pan.

In a heavy saucepan over moderate heat, melt together the sugar, butter, and chocolate. Set aside. Beat the eggs well and add vanilla and flour. Fold in the nuts and the warm chocolate mixture.

Bake 30 minutes, remove from the oven, and let cool on a rack.

1 cup sugar
8 tablespoons (1 stick) butter
3 squares bitter chocolate
3 eggs
1 teaspoon vanilla extract
⅓ cup flour
1 cup chopped nuts, such as almonds, hazelnuts, pecans, or walnuts

1 square bitter chocolate
A lump of butter the size of a walnut
1 cup confectioners' sugar
1 to 2 tablespoons warm milk
½ teaspoon vanilla extract

To make the frosting, melt the square of chocolate and the butter together in a heavy saucepan. Add the sugar and mix well. Add the milk and vanilla and mix again. Spread the frosting over the pan of brownies. Cut into 1- or 2-inch squares just before serving.

Serving Suggestions: The brownies are perfect picnic fare, with a basket of strawberries to nibble with them. In winter, serve the brownies with a big bowl of clementines.

Tips:
Do the melting in the microwave.

Toast the nuts in a 350° oven for about 5 minutes, or until they begin to smell delicious, for a nuttier flavor.

Variations:
Add a spoonful of instant espresso for mocha brownies; use only 2½ squares chocolate for the brownie batter.

Bake the brownies in a round pan, dust confectioners' sugar over the top when they've cooled, and cut into thin wedges to serve.

These sensational Italian cookies are from Siena, where they're a Christmas specialty. The cookies don't look very exciting—they're soft and pale—but if you like almonds, you'll love these.

Soft Almond Paste Cookies
(Ricciarelli)

Carol Field

MAKES 20 COOKIES

Grind the almonds to a fine powder in a nut grinder or food processor fitted with the steel blade. Transfer to a mixer bowl and mix in the almond paste with an electric mixer. Add the egg white and mix at the lowest speed until thoroughly blended. The dough should be firm. Add the baking powder; if you're using ammonium carbonate, crush it with the flat side of a cleaver to a powder and add to the almond paste. Add the vanilla and mix until well blended.

Transfer the dough to a floured surface and roll into a long log about ¾ inch in diameter. Slice the log at 2-inch intervals and shape each piece into a lozenge or diamond. Sift confectioners' sugar lightly over the shaped dough and flatten each piece slightly with a sugar-coated hand. Place the *ricciarelli* 1 inch apart on parchment-lined baking sheets and let stand, uncovered, at room temperature at least 1 hour or overnight.

Heat the oven to 300°. Bake until very light tan, 20 to 30 minutes. Cool on racks. Take care not to bake until brown or crisp; it is the softness that makes *ricciarelli* so delicious.

Serving Suggestion: These cookies are particularly delicious with an after-dinner wine (see the list on page 251) like the Italian vin santo.

1 cup blanched almonds
14 ounces almond paste
2 tablespoons egg white
½ teaspoon baking powder or
    ¼ teaspoon ammonium carbonate
1 teaspoon vanilla extract
Confectioners' sugar

Tips:

Don't line the pan with aluminum foil; it would give these cookies a little crust, which would spoil them.

Lightly grease the baking sheets if you can't find parchment paper.

Note: Parchment paper, an excellent liner for baking cookies, comes in rolls and standard pan-sized sheets and can be reused several times; it keeps baking pans free of the burned sugar and butter stains that eventually cause uneven baking. Look for parchment paper in specialty equipment stores; some large hardware stores have it too.

Toasted Hazelnut Cookies

Diane Rossen Worthington

¾ cup sliced or chopped hazelnuts
8 tablespoons (1 stick) unsalted butter,
    at room temperature
½ cup dark brown sugar
1 teaspoon vanilla extract
1 large egg
¾ cup all-purpose flour
Powdered sugar for garnish (optional)

Toasting the hazelnuts first makes all the difference in flavor for these very simple cookies. They're best eaten the day they're made.

MAKES 25 (2-INCH) COOKIES

Preheat the oven to 350°. Place the hazelnuts on a baking sheet and toast until light brown, 3 to 5 minutes. Remove from the oven and let cool.

In a medium mixing bowl, combine the butter and brown sugar and mix with an electric mixer until well blended. Add the vanilla and egg and then slowly incorporate the flour. Carefully stir in the toasted hazelnuts.

Increase the oven to 375°. Drop teaspoons of the batter 1 inch apart on 2 ungreased cookie sheets. Bake until the cookies are light brown, about 8 minutes. Place the cookies on cooling racks. Sprinkle cookies with powdered sugar, if desired.

Serving Suggestion: A plate of cookies is wonderful enough by itself, but we think it's really great to have a plate of several kinds of cookies. You can mix home-made ones and first-quality store-bought ones, some of which can be very good indeed. Having a choice seems extravagant; actually it's very little extra effort.

Tip: From Maida Heatter: Line the cookie sheet with aluminum foil anytime you're baking butter cookies (that is, crisp cookies); you won't have to grease the cookie sheet, the cookies won't stick, and as a bonus you don't have to wash the pan afterward.

Variation: Substitute ½ cup finely chopped unsalted cashews or ½ cup pine nuts for the hazelnuts. Substitute white sugar for the dark brown.

Pinch Pie

Irma Rombauer

This terrific meringue tart shell has been resurrected from the great first edition of The Joy of Cooking—*it's been dropped from later editions, probably thought to be too old-fashioned. But as Rombauer says, it's "a sure-fire hit . . . deserves all the asterisks in the printing press. I never serve it to newcomers without sending them home happy, replete, and with the recipe in their pockets." It has a satisfying meringue crunch with a soft, chewy interior. It's just the right foil for sliced sweetened fruit and whipped cream.*

SERVES 6

Sift:

1 cup sugar

Place on a platter:

3 egg whites

½ teaspoon any baking powder

⅛ teaspoon salt

Combine in a small pitcher or cup:

1 teaspoon vanilla

1 teaspoon vinegar

1 teaspoon water

*W*hip the egg whites by hand until they are very stiff. Add the sifted sugar very slowly, ½ teaspoonful at a time, alternately with a few drops of the combined liquids. Beat constantly. When all the ingredients have been added, continue to beat the meringue for several minutes.

When making meringue tart with an electric beater, combine all the ingredients except the sugar. Use high speed. When the egg whites are stiff, add the sugar, a tablespoonful at a time.

Heap it upon the lightly greased platter or dish from which it is to be served or in a pan with a removable rim. Subsequent baking will not affect the platter or dish. Or heap the meringue lightly onto an ovenproof plate or a piece of well-greased unglazed brown paper placed on a tin. Shape the meringue like a pie or tart with a heavy edge, using a spatula or knife. Bake it in a very slow oven, 275°, for 1 hour or longer. Remove the paper when the pie is cool. Slide the pie onto a platter or plate. When ready to serve the meringue, fill the center.

Serving Suggestions: The ideal filling is juicy ripe strawberries, lightly sugared and zipped up with a little lemon juice. Or briefly cook frozen strawberries, sieve the seeds out, and pour the puree over the strawberries to add color and flavor. Lemon Curd Mousse (page 221) is another good choice for a filling—it makes a kind of inside-out lemon meringue pie.

Tips:

Use an electric mixer; the meringue will go together very quickly.

Use superfine sugar instead of sifting the sugar.

Forget about making meringue on a humid day; it just won't work.

Add a touch of Crème de Cassis to the berries.

Marinate the berries in fresh orange juice.

From Nancy Silverton: Cut the strawberries horizontally if you're using berries whose flavor is disappointing; more of the surface is exposed, and more of the juice comes out.

EDITORS' KITCHEN

EASY PIE CRUSTS

For some of us, "easy as pie" is a cruel joke—sometimes the crust turns out perfectly, other times it's a disaster. Prepared pie crust mixes, dairy case crusts, or frozen shells aren't the only solutions; there are some excellent no-roll crusts that can be made fearlessly. One is a sweet press-in tart crust that's perfect for fruit tarts or pecan pie. All you need is an inexpensive tart pan with a removable bottom; the standard size is ten inches. Cookie-crumb crusts are also quite painless to put together. Frozen puff pastry also makes a good pie or tart crust.

Press-in Tart Crust

Mix together 1 cup plus 2 tablespoons unbleached white flour, 4 teaspoons sugar, and ⅛ teaspoon salt. Cut in 9 tablespoons unsalted butter using a pastry blender or the food processor. The mixture should have the texture of cornmeal. Add 4 teaspoons water and ½ teaspoon vanilla extract and continue to work it until the dough is a smooth and uniform texture and can be shaped into a ball. Line a 10-inch tart pan with a removable bottom by pressing the dough over the bottom and then up the sides. The sides should be about ¼ inch thick, even with the top of the pan, slightly thinner toward the base. You may need to fiddle with it a while, but don't worry, the crust will still be tender. Put the finished tart shell in the freezer to harden.

Preheat the oven to 400°. Prebake the frozen shell in the middle of the oven until it is lightly but evenly browned, about 12 minutes. Check during the baking: If the bottom is swelling anywhere, prick it with the tip of a knife and it will deflate. Remove from the oven, let cool, fill with fruit, and your pie is done. Or fill with a pecan filling while the crust is still warm.

Pecan Pie Filling

After baking the tart shell (see above), lower the oven temperature to 325°. Mix together 1 cup light corn syrup, 2 tablespoons melted butter, a pinch of salt, 3 lightly beaten eggs, 1 cup sugar, 1 teaspoon vanilla extract, and 1 cup pecan halves. Pour into the warm 10-

inch tart crust. Bake for 25 minutes. Remove from the oven and cool on a rack.

A cookie-crumb crust can be made with chocolate wafers, gingersnaps, zwieback, or amaretti.

Cookie-crumb Crusts

MAKES ONE 9-INCH PIE CRUST

Combine 8 tablespoons (1 stick) unsalted butter, melted, 3 tablespoons brown sugar, and a pinch of salt in a bowl. Add 2 cups fine cookie crumbs and mix well. Heavily butter a 9-inch pie pan. Spoon the crumbs into the pan and mold them evenly over the bottom and all the way up the sides.

Preheat the oven to 325°. Chill the pie shell for at least 15 minutes, then bake for 10 minutes, or until golden brown. Let cool before filling.

Here are some felicitous combinations of cookie crumbs and filling:

- Chocolate wafers with chocolate or coffee mousse

- Gingersnaps with Lemon Curd Mousse (page 221)

- Zwieback with blueberries heated with cinnamon and sugar to taste until they begin to pop; pour into the crust, top with a heated strawberry glaze, and chill.

- Amaretti with a chocolate glaze made by melting ½ cup chocolate chips in the microwave; drizzle glaze over cooled crust, refrigerate, and serve filled with ice cream.

You can also use any of the cookie crusts, except amaretti, for a no-bake cheesecake. Bake and cool the crust and fill it with this filling.

Crumb Crust Cheesecake

In a heavy-bottomed saucepan, mix ⅓ cup sugar, a pinch of salt, 1 tablespoon cornstarch, 1 cup milk, and 3 lightly beaten large eggs. Stir constantly over medium-low heat until thickened. Remove from heat and let cool. Beat 8 ounces cream cheese with 1 teaspoon vanilla, rum, almond, or orange extract until soft. Add the cooled milk mixture and blend until smooth. Pour the filling into a baked and cooled Cookie-crumb Crust (page 237) and chill for at least 4 hours.

Puff Pastry Crust

The Saucier puff pastry (the only brand made with butter) available in the supermarket freezer case comes in one sheet in a one-pound package. It is very easy to use for pie or tart shells and for individual pastries.

Defrost a pastry sheet until soft enough to roll out but still cold. Roll out into a square 2 to 3 inches wider than your pie pan. Line the pan, bringing the edges of the dough well over the rim of the pan since it will shrink in the baking. Prick the crust in several places—it will still swell up while it's baking, but don't worry, it will calm down later.

Preheat the oven to 450°. Put the pan in the oven and immediately lower the heat to 400°. Bake for 15 minutes. Let cool, spread with an almond paste base, if desired, and fill with fruit. Glaze the fruit or not, as you like.

Almond Base for Fruit Tarts

Mix 8 ounces almond paste with a well-beaten egg and enough butter to make it spreadable. Spread the mixture evenly over the bottom of a pie or tart shell before adding fruit.

Lemon Curd Napoleons

Defrost a sheet of frozen puff pastry until soft enough to handle but still cold. Roll out into a 12 × 17-inch rectangle, then cut into 2 × 5-inch rectangles (you should have 18 pieces). Bake as directed above. Let cool.

Assemble the napoleons on a large sheet of wax paper. Spread 1 pastry rectangle with Lemon Curd Mousse (page 221), top with a second rectangle, spread that with the mousse, then top with a third rectangle. Lightly dust with confectioners' sugar. Continue until all are assembled. Transfer each pastry to a serving plate, garnish with fresh berries and a mint leaf, and serve.

Chocolate– Chestnut Log

Deborah Madison

This festive dessert is wonderfully rich, easy to put together, and keeps very well. It's particularly nice for a holiday buffet, where it can stand in for the more traditional—and extremely labor-intensive—Yule log dessert, Bûche de Noël. The only trick here is to remember to buy the chestnut puree when you're in a gourmet store. Once you have it in the cupboard, you can whip up this dessert on a moment's notice with ingredients you usually have on hand.

Combine the chocolate and butter in a heavy saucepan and melt slowly over low heat. Stir occasionally to make sure it's not sticking and to break up the chocolate. Alternatively, melt the butter and chocolate in a double boiler.

Put the chestnut puree in a bowl. When the chocolate has melted, add it to the puree along with the rum. Whisk until the mixture is smooth and shiny, then stir in

5 ounces semisweet chocolate
¼ cup (1½ sticks) unsalted butter
1 1-pound can chestnut puree
1 tablespoon dark rum
1 cup walnut meats
Walnut halves for garnish
1 cup heavy cream
½ teaspoon vanilla extract

the walnuts. Cover and refrigerate until cool and firm, about 1½ hours.

Put a large piece of plastic wrap on the counter. Scrape the cool chestnut mixture onto it and shape it roughly into a log about 8 to 10 inches long. Fold the plastic tightly over the log, then shape it with your hands. Transfer to a flat plate and return it to the refrigerator until hardened, another 2 hours or so.

To serve, peel away the plastic wrap and set the log on a serving dish. Garnish it with the walnut halves. Whip the cream until it holds soft peaks and stir in the vanilla. Slice the log and serve each piece with a spoonful of cream on the side.

Serving Suggestion: For the holidays, serve it on a platter surrounded by sprigs of holly and evergreens.

Tip: Wrap the log in plastic wrap and refrigerate; it will keep for at least a week.

Variation: Decorate the log with glistening candied fruits alongside the walnut halves.

Chocolate–Amaretti Torte

Dorie Greenspan

The real magic here is the spectacular taste of this surprisingly simple torte. Even hopeless bakers can turn this one out perfectly. Our guests devoured this torte in even less time than it took to make it.

SERVES 10 TO 14

𝒫lace a rack in the center of the oven and preheat the oven to 350°. Butter an 8-inch round cake pan. Line the bottom with waxed paper and butter the paper. Dust the inside of the pan with flour and tap out the excess. Melt the chocolates in the top of a double boiler over hot water or in a bowl in a microwave; set aside.

Place the amaretti and almonds in a food processor and pulse several times, until the mixture is evenly ground. Turn out onto a sheet of wax paper and reserve. Put the butter, sugar, and eggs into the work bowl and process until the mixture is satiny smooth and no longer grainy, about 3 minutes. Stop to scrape the bowl occasionally to ensure that the batter is properly blended. Pour in the reserved amaretti–almond powder and the melted chocolate. Pulse just until the mixture is well combined.

Turn the batter into the prepared pan and bake 25 to 30 minutes. The cake will dome slightly and the top will look dry and, perhaps, cracked. Cool the cake on a rack for 30 minutes. Run a blunt knife around the edges of the pan and turn out the cake. Peel off the paper, invert, and cool right-side up on the rack. The cake is only about 1 inch high, but it packs a lot of taste.

This is at its best at room temperature. Dust the top with cocoa or confectioners' sugar, if desired, and cut into very thin slices. (It's richer than it looks.) Finish

1 ounce unsweetened chocolate

3 ounces high-quality bittersweet chocolate, such as Lindt or Tobler

6 large, double amaretti (Italian macaroons available in specialty stores and some supermarkets; look for the Saronno brand)

¾ cup sliced or julienned blanched almonds

8 tablespoons (1 stick) unsalted butter, at room temperature

½ cup sugar

3 large eggs, at room temperature

Cocoa or confectioners' sugar (optional)

Heavy cream, lightly whipped, or premium-quality vanilla or coffee ice cream

each plate with a small scoop of ice cream or spoonful of unsweetened, lightly whipped heavy cream.

Tips:
Dust the buttered pan with cocoa since this is a flourless cake and you won't have that canister out.

Wrap the cake in plastic wrap; it will keep for 3 days at room temperature or, wrapped airtight, for 1 month in the freezer.

Chocolate Sauce

Paula Wolfert after Michel Guérard

This luscious, rich-tasting chocolate sauce isn't actually very rich at all. It's a great emergency dessert; if you have ice cream on hand and cocoa in the cupboard, you can produce a half-homemade dessert in just a few minutes. The sauce keeps for two to three weeks in the refrigerator. Michel Guérard likes to serve it with honey ice cream, but it tastes just as good with plain American vanilla.

¾ cup sifted unsweetened cocoa
    powder (Droste's Dutch)
¾ cup sugar
Pinch of salt
1 cup cold water
2 tablespoons unsalted butter

MAKES ABOUT 2 CUPS

In a 6-cup saucepan, stir the cocoa, sugar, and salt together to mix. Add the water and stir until smooth. Place over medium heat and stir until the mixture comes to a low boil.

Let simmer 3 minutes. Add the butter, stir until melted, and simmer 3 minutes more. Serve tepid.

Tip: Use a large glass bowl or measuring cup to make the sauce in your microwave.

Variations:

Replace ¼ cup of the water with Kahlúa, Amaretto, Grand Marnier, or another liqueur of your choice for a more sophisticated dessert.

From Paula Wolfert: Add a pinch of cinnamon to the sauce during the final 3 minutes.

EDITORS' KITCHEN

Once you know about this recipe, we're sure you'll keep several bags of frozen berries in the freezer to make granita on a moment's notice.

Instant Berry Granita

SERVES 4

Freeze 2 pints of berries (strawberries, blueberries, or raspberries) in a single layer on a baking sheet. Keep the berries in the freezer until you're ready to make the granita. Put them in the food processor with ½ to ¾ cup superfine sugar, lemon juice to taste (about ½ lemon), and 1 tablespoon liqueur, if desired, and process until you have a good smooth texture. Serve immediately.

Tips:

Use Grand Marnier liqueur with blueberries, framboise with raspberries, Crème de Cassis with strawberries.

Make the granita with frozen blocks of sweetened berries, omitting the sugar; increase the amount of lemon juice and liqueur to taste.

Fresh Lime Ice Cream

Leslie Newman

If we had to have only one ice cream the rest of our lives, this would be it. Intensely limey, smooth but not too rich, this perfectly balanced dessert goes together in just moments. It's especially good after Mexican or Indian food, and of course it's the ideal ending to any summer meal. Just remember to start the ice cream the night before you want to serve it. Divide the recipe exactly in half if you have one of those small ice-cream makers; you will need about three limes, six for the larger quantity.

1 tablespoon plus 1 teaspoon grated lime zest

½ cup plus 1 tablespoon fresh lime juice

2 cups sugar, preferably superfine

Pinch of salt

2 cups heavy cream

2 cups milk

MAKES ABOUT 1½ QUARTS

In a large bowl, combine the lime zest, lime juice, sugar, and salt; stir to mix well.

Gradually add the cream and then the milk; stir gently until the sugar dissolves. Cover and refrigerate for at least 4 hours or overnight, if possible, to allow the flavor to develop fully.

Stir the mixture, pour it into an ice-cream maker, and freeze according to the manufacturer's instructions.

Tips:

Remove the zest before juicing the lime, using a zester to produce delicate strands; whiz these around in a minichopper.

Grind regular sugar to the right texture in the food processor if you don't have superfine sugar.

Pineapple in Port Wine

Diana Kennedy after Dione Lucas

This is a particularly good treatment for a pineapple that turns out not to be as sweet as it should be. The better the port, the better the dessert. Make this dessert a day ahead for the best flavor.

SERVES 4 TO 5

1 medium pineapple (about 2½
   pounds), cleaned
Finely pared zest of 1 orange
Finely pared zest of ½ grapefruit
4 tablespoons light brown sugar, or
   to taste
¾ cup pineapple juice
½ cup port

Peel, slice, and core the pineapple and cut into 1-inch cubes or thin slices. Julienne the citrus zests and put them in a pan together with the sugar and pineapple juice. Cook over a low flame until the zests are tender but not too soft, about 5 minutes. While the liquid is still warm, add the pineapple pieces and stir in the port. Set aside to macerate overnight or for at least 8 hours.

Serving Suggestions: The pineapple is delicious with a little cloud of unsweetened whipped cream or crème fraîche; it also makes a wonderful ice cream topping. And it's very good by itself.

Tips:

Let the pineapple come to room temperature before you serve it or the flavors will be lost.

Use a citrus zester to remove the orange and grapefruit peels and save yourself extra minutes.

Variation: Cut a really sweet pineapple into tiny cubes, chill very well, and pour a little chilled tequila over it just before serving. Decorate with mint sprigs. This Mexican idea for a hot-weather dessert also works well as a first course.

Mango Compote

Alice Waters

5 large ripe mangoes
About 2 teaspoons lime juice
2 cups Sauternes

This exotic, exhilarating dessert can be made just about any time of year, since different types of mangoes are constantly coming into the market.

SERVES 10

Peel the mangoes and slice them from the stones in about ⅜-inch slices. Put them in a shallow dish and sprinkle with 2 teaspoons lime juice. Pour 2 cups Sauternes over the mangoes, cover, and refrigerate for 2 to 3 hours. Remove them from the refrigerator 1 hour before serving and taste for lime juice. There should be a hint of lime flavor; add more juice if necessary.

Serving Suggestion: Little macaroons would be a perfect accompaniment for the compote.

Note: It's hard to choose good mangoes. Your best guide is your nose—choose the most fragrant ones. The little Asian ones are particularly good.

When you bring home some beautiful cherries that turn out to be a bit underripe, try Alice Waters' method of bringing out their flavor. The balsamic vinegar works miracles on cherries. This is one of the few cherry desserts we've seen that don't require you to spend a lot of time pitting them—but be sure to warn your guests that the pits are still there.

Alice's Cherry Compote with Balsamic Vinegar

Lindsey Shere after Alice Waters

SERVES 6

2 pounds black cherries
¼ cup sugar
1 teaspoon kirsch
2 to 3 teaspoons balsamic vinegar

Put the cherries in a colander, pick out any bad ones, rinse, and stem. Put them in one layer in a heavy-bottomed noncorroding sauté pan. If you haven't a pan big enough, cook the cherries in two or more batches. Sprinkle the fruit with the sugar and shake the pan over high heat for about 5 minutes, or until the sugar melts and the cherries feel a little soft when you press them. The sugar will make little white crystals on the cherries before it melts.

Sprinkle the cherries with the kirsch and vinegar and shake them for about 30 seconds longer. Scrape them with their juice into a container and chill or cool to room temperature, then let stand at least an hour or two.

Serving Suggestions: Serve the cherries in a sherbet glass or an old-fashioned round champagne glass, with a basket of amaretti on the side.

Variation: From Marcella Hazan: Rinse strawberries (with their stems intact, so they don't take on water), hull them, slice them in half if they're very large, sugar them to taste, and add just a little balsamic vinegar right before serving.

Fruit Compotes

On a buffet table, for brunch, after an extravagantly rich dinner, in the dog days of summer, the mixed fruit compote will always find plenty of fans. Be sure the fruits are either perfectly ripe and in season or exemplary of their type out of season. Combinations we find interesting include tropical fruits, mixed melons with a sprinkling of fresh mint, mixed berries, strawberries with oranges, even several kinds of grapes. It's almost impossible to go wrong. What makes these mixtures really sparkle is the addition of lemon or lime juice, orange flower water, chopped mint, dessert wines, or citrus zest. Here are some ideas from the experts:

- From Diana Kennedy: Add a little orange zest.

- From Paula Wolfert: Add a jolt of orzat, the Italian almond syrup.

- From Elizabeth David: Add a splash of port to strawberries.

- From Angelo Pelligrini: Float just-picked strawberries and raspberries together in sweet sherry.

- From Elizabeth David: Dress a mixed fruit salad with strawberry or raspberry puree mixed with champagne for a traditional Russian summer compote.

- From Martha Rose Shulman: Add finely chopped mint and a spoonful of Grand Marnier to orange sections.

- From Eugene Walter: Slice ripe peaches (better yet white peaches), add white port, lemon juice, and sugar to taste, and serve chilled.

Antiguan Charcoal-baked Bananas

Maggie Waldron

This unusual Caribbean dessert can be started in the leftover coals while your guests are finishing their grilled dinner. The bananas are just as delicious made in the coals of a winter fire indoors.

SERVES 6

Set the bunch of unpeeled bananas in hot coals. Bake until black and soft to the touch. Meanwhile, heat butter with brown sugar and spice until bubbly. Each person should slit his banana, squeeze a lime half over it, and drizzle the butter-sugar mixture on top. Ignite rum and pour it flaming over the bananas a little at a time, shaking the skillet gently until the flame dies.

Serving Suggestion: This is an ideal dessert to serve a crowd at a barbecue. It multiplies very well, and the guests themselves put the dessert together.

Tip: Remove the bananas when they're soft and shiny, about 5 minutes in the hot coals.

6 large ripe bananas, in 1 bunch
4 tablespoons butter
½ cup brown sugar
½ teaspoon ground allspice or ½ teaspoon freshly grated nutmeg
3 limes, halved
¼ cup dark rum, heated in a small pan placed on the grill

Dried Apricots Baked with Vanilla

Deborah Madison

1 cup dried apricots
1 cup warm water
1 1-inch piece vanilla bean, sliced in half lengthwise
1 tablespoon sugar

In the middle of winter, these apricots are pure sunshine—simple and perfect. The apricots plump up and become perfumed with the vanilla seeds. This is an ideal impromptu dessert.

SERVES 6

Preheat the oven to 350°. Cover the apricots with the warm water and let them stand for 15 minutes if they are already plump and soft, 30 minutes if they are hard to begin with. Drain and reserve the water.

Put the water and vanilla bean in a baking dish—an 8-inch pie plate is just right. Scrape out the seeds of the vanilla bean with the tip of a knife and break them up in the water. Add the apricots, sprinkle them with the sugar, cover with foil, and bake until the water is nearly absorbed, about 1 hour. Turn each of the apricots over in the syrup, then cover and refrigerate. Serve chilled.

Serving Suggestions: If you can get Greek yogurt in your area, the chilled apricots are delicious with it—or with any thick yogurt, or fresh ricotta. For a fancier treatment, try the apricots with Coeur à la Crème (page 220), minus the raspberry sauce. The apricots are just as tasty for breakfast as for dessert, especially with yogurt.

Tip: Allow 4 or 5 apricots per serving; 1 cup, about ½ pound, equals about 25 small apricots.

EDITORS' KITCHEN

If you want something just a little sweet to end the meal, consider skipping the traditional dessert course. Instead, bring out a selection of sweet tidbits and a dessert wine. Even petit fours are making a comeback as the only dessert at the most elegant dinner parties. Most of us are delighted not to be deeply tempted but, like children, we don't want to have no treats at all. All of these goodies can be kept on hand for emergency dinner parties.

DESSERT WINES

Dessert wines should be served in small glasses—a little goes a long way. Serve the white wines cold. Sweet wines are excellent foils for goat cheese or other intense, salty cheeses.

- Prosecco amabile, an Italian version of champagne

- Very dry champagne, with or without something in it, such as one perfect strawberry or a canned apricot that's been soaking in brandy for a couple of hours. Drop the fruit into a wide champagne glass, fill with champagne, and tuck a sprig of mint on the edge of the glass. Serve with crisp cookies.

- Beaumes de Venise, a heavenly sweet French wine

- Vin santo, the sweet Italian wine

- Sauternes or muscat

- Essensia, the lovely orange-scented California muscat

- Port, red or white

TIDBITS

These sweet tidbits are great with coffee, reminiscent of the little treats you're served at the end of a meal in the best French restaurants.

- Chocolate truffles, chocolate-covered espresso beans, mints

- Nutmeats, plain, toasted, spiced, glazed, minted, or candy-coated

- Dried fruits, such as those outrageous Australian glazed apricots, or Bing cherries, or wild blueberries, or whatever your market has to offer

- Fresh dates or candied citrus peels or crystallized peels

- Exotica like fresh lichee nuts or brandied cherries

- Finger fruits, such as long-stemmed strawberries, clementines, or the perfect small pear

- Elegant little cookies or crisps, Shortbread (page 228), or Italian biscotti, or amarettini or baby macaroons piled in little baskets

Acknowledgments

Every effort has been made to ascertain the ownership of all copyrighted material and to secure the necessary permissions. In the event of any questions arising as to the use of any material, the editor and the publishers, while expressing regret for any inadvertent error, will be happy to make the necessary correction in future printings.

Grateful acknowledgment is made to the publishers listed below for permission to reprint their copyrighted material:

Sweet Pea Guacamole from *Secret Ingredients* by Michael Roberts. Copyright © 1988 by Michael Roberts. Used by permission of Bantam Books, a division of Bantam, Doubleday, Dell Publishing Group, Inc.

Mushroom and Hazelnut Soup from *The Mediterranean Kitchen* by Joyce Goldstein. Copyright © 1989 by Joyce Goldstein. Reprinted by permission of William Morrow and Company, Inc.

Yellow Squash Soup from *The Taste of Summer* by Diane Rossen Worthington. Copyright © 1988 by Diane Rossen Worthington. Used by permission of Bantam Books, a division of Bantam, Doubleday, Dell Publishing Group, Inc.

Cold Tomato Soup from *The New York Times Cookbook* edited by Craig Claiborne. Copyright © 1961 by Craig Claiborne. Reprinted by permission of HarperCollins Publishers, Inc.

Fresh Coriander Soup (*Sopa de Coentro*) from *The Food of Portugal* by Jean Anderson. Copyright © 1986 by Jean Anderson. Reprinted by permission of William Morrow and Company, Inc.

Cold Buttermilk Soup from *The Art of Eating* by M. F. K. Fisher. Copyright 1937, 1941, 1942, 1943, 1948, 1949, 1954 by M. F. K. Fisher, renewed © 1971, 1976, 1977 by Mary Kennedy Friede. Reprinted by permission of Macmillan Publishing Company, Inc.

Billi Bi from *The New York Times Cookbook* edited by Craig Claiborne. Copyright © 1961 by Craig Claiborne. Reprinted by permission of HarperCollins Publishers, Inc.

Oyster Avgolemono Soup from *Town and Country Cookbook* by James Villas. Copyright © 1985 by James Villas. Reprinted by permission of Little, Brown and Company, Inc.

Piquant Prawns (*Gambas Picantes*) from *Madhur Jaffrey's World of the East Vegetarian Cooking* by Madhur Jaffrey. Copyright © 1981 by Madhur Jaffrey. Reprinted by permission of Alfred A. Knopf, Inc.

Bourbon Shrimp from *Cooking with the New American Chefs* edited by Ellen Brown. Copyright © 1985 by Ellen Brown. Reprinted by permission of HarperCollins Publishers, Inc.

Bay Scallops with Sautéed Apples from *The Wolfgang Puck Cookbook* by Wolfgang Puck. Copyright © 1986 by Wolfgang Puck. Reprinted by permission of Random House, Inc.

Pasta with Caviar (*Pasta con caviale*) from *The Authentic Pasta Book* by Fred Plotkin. Copyright © 1985 by Fred Plotkin. Reprinted by permission of Simon and Schuster, Inc.

Cappellini with Lemon and Basil from *The Savory Way* by Deborah Madison. Copyright © 1990 by Deborah Madison. Used by permission of Bantam Books, a division of Bantam, Doubleday, Dell Publishing Group, Inc.

Celery Hearts with Peppercorn Dressing from *Classic Chinese Cuisine* by Nina Simonds. Copyright © 1982 by Nina Simonds. Reprinted by permission of Houghton Mifflin Company, Inc.

Thai Cucumber Salad from *Feasts* by Leslie Newman. Copyright © 1990 Leslie Newman. Reprinted by permission of HarperCollins Publishers, Inc.

Mushroom and Cheese Salad (*Insalata di funghi e formaggio*) from *The Classic Italian Cookbook* by Marcella Hazan, translated by Victor Hazan. Copyright © 1973 by Marcella Hazan and Victor Hazan. Reprinted by permission of Alfred A. Knopf, Inc.

Shrimp with Cashew Nuts from *Fragrant Harbor Taste* by Ken Hom. Copyright © 1989 by Taurom, Inc. Reprinted by permission of Simon and Schuster, Inc.

Cape Scallops Sautéed with Garlic and Sun-dried Tomatoes from *Jasper White's Cooking for New England* by Jasper White. Copyright © 1988 by Jasper White. Reprinted by permission of HarperCollins Publishers, Inc.

Portuguese Crab Cakes with Mint and Cilantro (*Bolinhos de Santola*) from *The Mediterranean Kitchen* by Joyce Goldstein. Copyright © 1989 by Joyce Goldstein. Reprinted by permission of William Morrow and Company, Inc.

Salmon Slices with Walnut or Hazelnut Vinaigrette (*Tranches de saumon tièdes à la vinaigrette de noix ou de noisettes*) from *In Madeleine's Kitchen* by Madeleine Kamman. Copyright © 1984 by Madeleine Kamman. Reprinted by permission of Atheneum Publishers, an imprint of Macmillan Publishing Company, Inc.

Grilled Swordfish with Mustard from *City Cuisine* by Susan Feniger and Mary Sue Milliken. Copyright © 1988 by Susan Feniger and Mary Sue Milliken. Reprinted by permission of William Morrow and Company, Inc.

Baked Cod with Onions and Mint (*Merluzzo all'istriana*) from *The Mediterranean Kitchen* by Joyce Goldstein. Copyright © 1989 by Joyce Goldstein. Reprinted by permission of William Morrow and Company, Inc.

Catfish Baked with Cheese from *Craig Claiborne's Southern Cooking.* Copyright © 1987 by Clamshell Productions, Inc. Reprinted by permission of Times Books, a division of Random House, Inc.

Chicken Broiled with Mustard, Herbs, and Bread Crumbs (*Poulets grillés à la diable*) from *Mastering the Art of French Cooking, Vol. I* by Julia Child, Simone Beck, and Louisette Bertholle. Copyright © 1961 by Alfred A. Knopf, Inc. Reprinted by permission of Alfred A. Knopf, Inc.

Orange-spiced Chicken Wings from *The Maple Syrup Cookbook* by Ken Haedrich. Copyright © 1989 by Ken Haedrich. Reprinted by permission of Storey Communications, Inc.

Bangkok Chicken from *Pacific Flowers: Oriental Recipes for a Contemporary Kitchen* by Hugh Carpenter. Copyright © 1988 by Hugh Carpenter. Reprinted by permission of Stewart, Tabori and Chang Publishers, Inc.

Oven-fried Chicken from *Cooking from Quilt Country* by Marcia Adams. Copyright © 1989 by Marcia Adams. Reprinted by permission of Clarkson N. Potter, Inc.

Braised Chicken Thighs with Spicy Tomato and Ginger Sauce from *Ken Hom's East Meets West Cuisine* by Ken Hom. Copyright © 1987 by Taurom, Inc. Reprinted by permission of Simon and Schuster, Inc.

Rolled Stuffed Turkey Cutlets (*Involtini di tacchino*) from *Giuliano Bugialli's Foods of Italy* by Giuliano Bugialli. Copyright © 1984 by Giuliano Bugialli. Reprinted by permission of Stewart, Tabori and Chang Publishers, Inc.

Grilled Beef Tenderloin with Roquefort and Red Pepper Butter from *The Heritage of Southern Cooking* by Camille Glenn. Copyright © 1986 by Camille Glenn. Reprinted by permission of Workman Publishing Company, Inc.

Grilled Flank Steak on a Bed of Roasted Peppers and Onions from *The Mediterranean Kitchen* by Joyce Goldstein. Copyright © 1989 by Joyce Goldstein. Reprinted by permission of William Morrow and Company, Inc.

Spicy Skirt Steak with Cinnamon from *Secret Ingredients* by Michael Roberts. Copyright © 1988 by Michael Roberts. Used by permission of Bantam Books, a division of Bantam, Doubleday, Dell Publishing Group, Inc.

Beef Braised in Coffee (*Stracotto al Caffè*) from *Italian Cooking in the Grand Tradition* by Jo Bettoja and Anna Maria Cornetto. Copyright © 1982 by Jo Bettoja and Anna Maria Cornetto. Reprinted by permission of Curtis Brown, Ltd.

Wild Mushroom Meat Loaf from *Country Food: A Seasonal Journal* by Miriam Ungerer. Copyright © 1982, 1983 by Miriam Ungerer. Reprinted by permission of Random House, Inc.

Veal Scallops with Fennel (*Escalopes de veau au fenouil*) from *Elizabeth David Classics: Mediterranean Food, French Country Cooking, Summer Cooking.* Copyright © 1980 by Elizabeth David. Reprinted by permission of Alfred A. Knopf, Inc.

Roast Pork with Bay Leaves (*Arrosto di maiale all'alloro*) from *The Classic Italian Cookbook* by Marcella Hazan. Copyright © 1973 by Marcella Hazan and Victor Hazan. Reprinted by permission of Alfred A. Knopf, Inc.

Succulent Pork Roast with Fennel (*Arista*) from *Cucina Rustica* by Viana La Place and Evan Kleiman. Copyright © 1990 by Viana La Place and Evan Kleiman. Reprinted by permission of William Morrow and Company, Inc.

Sicilian Meatballs with Raisins and Pine Nuts (*Polpette alla siciliana*) from *Italian Cooking in the Grand Tradition* by

Jo Bettoja and Anna Maria Cornetto. Copyright © 1982 by Jo Bettoja and Anna Maria Cornetto. Reprinted by permission of Curtis Brown, Ltd.

Ham Baked in Cola from *American Cookery* by James Beard. Copyright © 1972 by James Beard. Reprinted by permission of Little, Brown and Company, Inc.

Church-Supper Ham Loaf from *Cooking from Quilt Country* by Marcia Adams. Copyright © 1989 by Marcia Adams. Reprinted by permission of Clarkson N. Potter, Inc.

Roast Lamb with Monsieur Henny's Potato, Onion, and Tomato Gratin (*Gigot rôti au gratin de Monsieur Henny*) adapted from *Bistro Cooking* by Patricia Wells. Copyright © 1989 by Patricia Wells. Reprinted by permission of Workman Publishing Company, Inc. All rights reserved.

Moghul Roasted Leg of Lamb (*Raan Saag*) from *One Dish Meals of Asia* by Jennifer Brennan. Copyright © 1991 by Jennifer Brennan. Reprinted by permission of HarperCollins Publishers, Inc.

Rack of Lamb with Anise and Sweet Garlic from *Cooking the Nouvelle Cuisine in America* by Michele Urvater and David Liederman. Copyright © 1979 by Michele Urvater and David Liederman. Reprinted by permission of Workman Publishing Company, Inc.

Lamb and Olive Balls from *The Feast of the Olive* by Maggie Blyth Klein. Copyright © 1983 by Addison-Wesley Publishing Company, Inc. Reprinted by permission of Addison-Wesley Publishing Company, Inc.

Pasta with Gorgonzola from *The Savory Way* by Deborah Madison. Copyright © 1990 by Deborah Madison. Used by permission of Bantam Books, a division of Bantam, Doubleday, Dell Publishing Group, Inc.

Pasta with Vodka (*Pasta alla wodka*) from *Italian Cooking in the Grand Tradition* by Jo Bettoja and Anna Maria Cornetto. Copyright © 1982 by Jo Bettoja and Anna Maria Cornetto. Reprinted by permission of Curtis Brown, Ltd.

Pasta with Eggplant Sauce (*Pasta alle melanzane*) from *Bugialli on Pasta* by Giuliano Bugialli. Copyright © 1988 by Giuliano Bugialli Enterprises, Inc. Reprinted by permission of Simon and Schuster, Inc.

Clams, Gremolata, and Linguine from *Chez Panisse Pasta, Pizza, and Calzone* by Alice Waters, Patricia Curtan, et al. Copyright © 1984 by Tango Rose, Inc. Reprinted by permission of Random House, Inc.

Pasta with Crabmeat (*Vermicelli ai granchi*) from *Bugialli on Pasta* by Giuliano Bugialli. Copyright © 1988 by Giuliano Bugialli Enterprises, Inc. Reprinted by permission of Simon and Schuster, Inc.

Asparagus Poêlé from *Jasper White's Cooking from New England* by Jasper White. Copyright © 1988 by Jasper White. Reprinted by permission of HarperCollins Publisher, Inc.

Baked Red Beets (*Rape rosse al forno*) from *More Classic Italian Cooking* by Marcella Hazan. Copyright © 1978 by Marcella Hazan and Victor Hazan. Reprinted by permission of Alfred A. Knopf, Inc.

Broccoli Smothered in Garlic Oil (*Hare gobhi ki sabzi*) from *Classic Indian Cooking* by Julie Sahni. Copyright © 1980 by Julie Sahni. Reprinted by permission of William Morrow and Company, Inc.

Shredded Brussels Sprouts from *City Cuisine* by Susan Feniger and Mary Sue Milliken. Copyright © 1988 by Susan Feniger and Mary Sue Milliken. Reprinted by permission of William Morrow and Company, Inc.

Sweet and Sour Red Cabbage from *City Cuisine* by Susan Feniger and Mary Sue Milliken. Copyright © 1988. Reprinted by permission of William Morrow and Company, Inc.

Wondrous Carrots from *The Heritage of Southern Cooking* by Camille Glenn. Copyright © 1986 by Camille Glenn. Reprinted by permission of Workman Publishing Company, Inc.

Cauliflower with Raisins and Pine Nuts (*Cavolfiore con l'uvetta e i pignoli*) from *Marcella's Italian Kitchen* by Marcella Hazan. Copyright © 1986 by Marcella Polini Hazan and Victor Hazan. Reprinted by permission of Alfred A. Knopf, Inc.

Pureed Celery Root with Apples (*Purée de céleri-rave aux pommes*) from *The Cooking of Southwest France* by Paula Wolfert. Copyright © 1983 by Paula Wolfert. Used by permission of Doubleday, a division of Bantam, Doubleday, Dell Publishing Group, Inc.

Corn Fritters from *Café Beaujolais* by Margaret Fox. Copyright © 1984 by Margaret Fox. Reprinted by permission of Ten Speed Press, Berkeley, California.

Early Summer Fresh Corn Pudding from *The Heritage of Southern Cooking* by Camille Glenn. Copyright © 1986 by Camille Glenn. Reprinted by permission of Workman Publishing Company, Inc.

Sweet and Sour Eggplant from *City Cuisine* by Susan Feniger and Mary Sue Milliken. Copyright © 1988 by

Susan Feniger and Mary Sue Milliken. Reprinted by permission of William Morrow and Company, Inc.

Baked Eggplant (*Melanzane al forno*) from *Italian Cooking in the Grand Tradition* by Jo Bettoja and Anna Maria Cornetto. Copyright © 1982 by Jo Bettoja and Anna Maria Cornetto. Reprinted by permission of Curtis Brown, Ltd.

Sautéed Fennel with Lemon from *Uncommon Fruits and Vegetables* by Elizabeth Schneider. Copyright © 1986 by Elizabeth Schneider. Reprinted by permission of HarperCollins Publishers, Inc.

Braised Garlic and String Beans from *Greene on Greens* by Bert Greene. Copyright © 1984 by Bert Greene. Reprinted by permission of Workman Publishing Company, Inc.

Stir-fried Green Beans from *The Key to Chinese Cooking* by Irene Kuo. Copyright © 1977 by Irene Kuo. Reprinted by permission of Alfred A. Knopf, Inc.

Tawny Mushroom Caps from *More Taste Than Time* by Abby Mandel. Copyright © 1988 by Machine Cuisine, Inc. Reprinted by permission of Simon and Schuster, Inc.

Sautéed-Braised Chanterelles from *Uncommon Fruits and Vegetables* by Elizabeth Schneider. Copyright © 1986 by Elizabeth Schneider. Reprinted by permission of HarperCollins Publishers, Inc.

Big Baked Onions from *The Way to Cook* by Julia Child. Copyright © 1989 by Julia Child. Reprinted by permission of Alfred A. Knopf, Inc.

Roasted Onions with Sage from *The Savory Way* by Deborah Madison. Copyright © 1990 by Deborah Madison. Used by permission of Bantam Books, a division of Bantam, Doubleday, Dell Publishing Group, Inc.

Pureed Parsnips from *James Beard's Theory and Practice of Good Cooking* by James Beard. Copyright © 1977 by James Beard. Reprinted by permission of Alfred A. Knopf, Inc.

Peas and Cucumber in Dill from *The Brilliant Bean* by Sally and Martin Stone. Copyright © 1988 by Sally Stone and Martin Stone. Used by permission of Bantam Books, a division of Bantam, Doubleday, Dell Publishing Group, Inc.

Slivered Snow Peas and Toasted Almonds (*Mange-tout aux amandes grillées*) from *In Madeleine's Kitchen* by Madeleine Kamman. Copyright © 1984 by Madeleine Kamman. Reprinted by permission of Atheneum

Publishers, an imprint of Macmillan Publishing Company, Inc.

Potato Gratin from *Mediterranean Light* by Martha Rose Shulman. Copyright © 1989 by Martha Rose Shulman. Used by permission of Bantam Books, a division of Bantam, Doubleday, Dell Publishing Group, Inc.

Baked Peppers, Potatoes, and Onions from *The Victory Garden Cookbook* by Marian Morash. Copyright © 1982 by Marian Morash and WGBH Educational Foundation. Reprinted by permission of Alfred A. Knopf, Inc.

Herbed New Potatoes with Vermouth from *The Taste of Summer* by Diane Rossen Worthington. Copyright © 1988 by Diane Rossen Worthington. Used by permission of Bantam Books, a division of Bantam, Doubleday, Dell Publishing Group, Inc.

Hot Devil Potatoes (*Patate al diavolicchio*) from *The Food of Southern Europe* by Carlo Middione. Copyright © 1987 by Carlo Middione. Reprinted by permission of William Morrow and Company, Inc.

Potato Cakes (*Tortitas de papa*) from *The Art of Mexican Cooking* by Diana Kennedy. Copyright © 1989 by Diana Kennedy. Used by permission of Bantam Books, a division of Bantam, Doubleday, Dell Publishing Group, Inc.

Red Radishes Sautéed with Vinegar (*Radis roses sautés au vinaigre*) from *In Madeleine's Kitchen* by Madeleine Kamman. Copyright © 1984 by Madeleine Kamman. Reprinted by permission of Atheneum Publishers, an imprint of Macmillan Publishing Company, Inc.

Skillet Scallions from *The Taste of Country Cooking* by Edna Lewis. Copyright © 1976 by Edna Lewis. Reprinted by permission of Alfred A. Knopf, Inc.

Spinach and Pear Puree (*La Mousseline d'épinards aux poires*) from *Roger Vergé's Entertaining in the French Style* by Roger Vergé. Copyright © 1986 by Flammarion. Reprinted by permission of Stewart, Tabori and Chang, Inc.

Slow-baked Tomatoes from *Mediterranean Light* by Martha Rose Shulman. Copyright © 1989 by Martha Rose Shulman. Used by permission of Bantam Books, a division of Bantam, Doubleday, Dell Publishing Group, Inc.

Turnips à la Comtesse from *Delectable Dishes from Termite Hall* by Eugene Walter. Copyright © 1982 by Eugene Walter. Reprinted by permission of Eugene Walter.

Stir-fried Zucchini with Sesame Seeds (*Hobak namul*)

from *Madhur Jaffrey's World of the East Vegetarian Cooking* by Madhur Jaffrey. Copyright © 1981 by Madhur Jaffrey. Reprinted by permission of Alfred A. Knopf, Inc.

Zucchini Stuffed with Corn and Cheese from *The Victory Garden Cookbook* by Marian Morash. Copyright © 1982 by Marian Morash and WGBH Educational Foundation. Reprinted by permission of Alfred A. Knopf, Inc.

Ten-minute Black Beans with Tomatoes and Coriander from *The Brilliant Bean* by Sally and Martin Stone. Copyright © 1988 by Sally Stone and Martin Stone. Used by permission of Bantam Books, a division of Bantam, Doubleday, Dell Publishing Group, Inc.

Lentil Puree from *American Cookery* by James Beard. Copyright © 1972 by James A. Beard. Reprinted by permission of Little, Brown and Company, Inc.

Spinach Pilaf from *City Cuisine* by Susan Feniger and Mary Sue Milliken. Copyright © 1988. Reprinted by permission of William Morrow and Company, Inc.

Saffron Risotto from *The Microwave Gourmet* by Barbara Kafka. Copyright © 1989. Reprinted by permission of William Morrow and Company, Inc.

Spoon Bread from *In Pursuit of Flavor* by Edna Lewis. Copyright © 1988 by Edna Lewis. Reprinted by permission of Alfred A. Knopf, Inc.

Custard-filled Cornbread from *The Breakfast Book* by Marion Cunningham. Copyright © 1987 by Marion Cunningham. Reprinted by permission of Alfred A. Knopf, Inc.

Spiced Masa Muffins from *More Taste Than Time* by Abby Mandel. Copyright © 1988 by Machine Cuisine, Inc. Reprinted by permission of Simon and Schuster, Inc.

Southern Biscuit Muffins from *Craig Claiborne's Southern Cooking* by Craig Claiborne. Copyright © 1987 by Clamshell Productions, Inc. Reprinted by permission of Times Books, a division of Random House, Inc.

Cream Biscuits from *Beard on Bread* by James Beard. Copyright © 1973 by James Beard. Reprinted by permission of Alfred A. Knopf, Inc.

Banana Nut Bread from *City Cuisine* by Susan Feniger and Mary Sue Milliken. Copyright © 1988. Reprinted by permission of William Morrow and Company, Inc.

American Bean Bread from *Biscuits, Spoonbread and Sweet Potato Pie* by Bill Neal. Copyright © 1990 by Bill Neal. Reprinted by permission of Alfred A. Knopf, Inc.

Icelandic Three-grain Brown Bread (*Brunbraud*) from *The Great Scandinavian Baking Book* by Beatrice Ojakangas. Copyright © 1988 by Beatrice Ojakangas. Reprinted by permission of Little, Brown and Company, Inc.

Cheese Crackers from *The Wooden Spoon Bread Book* by Marilyn M. Moore. Copyright © 1987 by Marilyn M. Moore. Reprinted by permission of Atlantic Monthly Press, Inc.

Coeur à la Crème with Raspberry Sauce from The Inn At Little Washington. Reprinted by permission of Patrick O'Connell.

Lemon Curd Mousse from *The Arcadia Cookbook* by Anne Rosenzweig. Copyright © 1986 by Harry N. Abrams, Inc. Reprinted by permission of Harry N. Abrams, Inc. All rights reserved.

Baked Maple Custard from *The Maple Syrup Cookbook* by Ken Haedrich. Copyright © 1989 by Ken Haedrich. Reprinted by permission of Storey Communications, Inc.

Panettone Bread Pudding from *Chez Panisse Cooking* by Alice Waters and Paul Bertholli. Copyright © 1988 by Alice Waters and Paul Bertholli. Reprinted by permission of Random House, Inc.

Blueberry Gingerbread from *Country Cakes* by Lisa Yockelson. Copyright © 1989 by Lisa Yockelson. Reprinted by permission of HarperCollins Publishers, Inc.

Gingersnap Dessert from *Nothing Fancy* by Diana Kennedy. Copyright © 1984 by Diana Kennedy. Reprinted by permission of Lescher & Lescher, Ltd.

Bittersweet Brownies by Jo Bettoja. Copyright © 1992 by Jo Bettoja. Printed by permission of Jo Bettoja and Curtis Brown, Ltd.

Soft Almond Paste Cookies (*Ricciarelli*) from *The Italian Baker* by Carol Field. Copyright © 1986 by Carol Field. Reprinted by permission of HarperCollins Publishers, Inc.

Toasted Hazelnut Cookies from *The Taste of Summer* by Diane Rossen Worthington. Copyright © 1988 by Diane Rossen Worthington. Used by permission of Bantam Books, a division of Bantam, Doubleday, Dell Publishing Group, Inc.

Pinch Pie from *Joy of Cooking* by Irma S. Rombauer and Marion Rombauer Becker. Copyright 1931, 1936, 1941, 1942, 1943, 1946, 1951, 1952, 1953, © 1962, 1963, 1964, 1975 by Bobbs-Merrill. Reprinted by permission of Macmillan Publishing Company, Inc.

Chocolate-Chestnut Log from *The Savory Way* by Deborah Madison. Copyright © 1990 by Deborah Madison. Reprinted by permission of Bantam Books, a division of Bantam, Doubleday, Dell Publishing Group, Inc.

Chocolate-Amaretti Torte from *Sweet Times* by Dorie Greenspan. Copyright © 1991 by Dorie Greenspan. Reprinted by permission of William Morrow and Company, Inc.

Michel Guérard's recipe for Chocolate Sauce from *The Cooking of South Western France Cookbook* by Paula Wolfert. Copyright © 1983 by Paula Wolfert. Used by permission of Doubleday, a division of Bantam, Doubleday, Dell Publishing Group, Inc.

Fresh Lime Ice Cream from *Feasts* by Leslie Newman. Copyright © 1990 by Leslie Newman. Reprinted by permission of HarperCollins Publishers, Inc.

Pineapple in Port Wine from *Nothing Fancy* by Diana Kennedy. Copyright © 1984 by Diana Kennedy. Reprinted by permission of Lescher & Lescher, Ltd.

Mango Compote from *Chez Panisse Cookbook* by Alice Waters. Copyright © 1982 by Alice Waters. Reprinted by permission of Random House, Inc.

Alice's Cherry Compote with Balsamic Vinegar from *Chez Panisse Desserts* by Lindsey Remolif Shere. Copyright © 1985 by Lindsey Remolif Shere. Reprinted by permission of Random House, Inc.

Antiguan Charcoal-baked Bananas from *Barbecue and Smoke Cooking* by Maggie Waldron. Copyright © 1978. Reprinted by permission of Maggie Waldron.

Dried Apricots Baked with Vanilla from *The Savory Way* by Deborah Madison. Copyright © 1990 by Deborah Madison. Used by permission of Bantam Books, a division of Bantam, Doubleday, Dell Publishing Group, Inc.

Index